JULES & GREG'S
WILD SWIM

JULES & GREG'S
WILD SWIM

THE DEEP-DIVE COMPANION TO THE HIT TV SERIES

JULIE WILSON NIMMO & GREG HEMPHILL

Black&White

Black&White

First published in the UK in 2025 by Black & White Publishing
An imprint of Bonnier Books UK
5th Floor, HYLO, 105 Bunhill Row,
London, EC1Y 8LZ

Copyright © Jules Wilson Nimmo & Greg Hemphill 2025
Photography credits are listed on page 228

All rights reserved.
No part of this publication may be reproduced,
stored or transmitted in any form by any means, electronic,
mechanical, photocopying or otherwise, without the
prior written permission of the publisher.

The right of Jules Wilson Nimmo & Greg Hemphill to be identified as Authors of this
work has been asserted by them in accordance with the
Copyright, Designs and Patents Act, 1988.

Jules & Greg's WILD SWIM isn't a guide to swimming safety and therefore neither the authors nor
the publisher can accept any responsibility for damage of any kind, to property or persons, that
occurs either directly or indirectly from the use of this book or from any wild swimming activity.

The publisher has made every reasonable effort to contact copyright holders of images and
other material. Any errors are inadvertent and anyone who for any reason has not been contacted
is invited to write to the publisher so that a full acknowledgement can be made in subsequent
editions of this work.

A CIP catalogue record for this book is available from the British Library.

ISBN: 978 1 78530 854 3

1 3 5 7 9 10 8 6 4 2

Layout by creativelink.tv
Printed and bound in Latvia

The authorised representative in the EEA is
Bonnier Books UK (Ireland) Limited.
Registered office address: Floor 3, Block 3, Miesian Plaza,
Dublin 2, D02 Y754, Ireland
compliance@bonnierbooks.ie

www.bonnierbooks.co.uk

FOR OUR PARENTS

Joan, Bill, Anne and Eddie x

JULES & GREG'S
WILD SWIM

WELCOME	01
1 DOCTOR'S ORDERS	25
2 SISTERS ARE DOING IT FOR THEMSELVES (AND THEIR HEALTH)	55
3 THE TROUBLE WITH MEN	69
4 SOUL SOOTHING	81
5 ON THE TIDES OF GRIEF AND LOSS	99
6 YOUR SECOND CHILDHOOD	111
7 THE MAGIC CURE: COMMUNITY	161
8 JUMP IN – THE WATER'S GREAT!	177
9 BEFORE YOU DIVE IN	185
10 GREG'S TIDE CHAT	213
BONUS CHAPTER: BONNIE SCOTLAND	221
ACKNOWLEDGEMENTS	229
ABOUT THE AUTHORS	230

ABOUT THE AUTHORS

Greg is an actor, writer, presenter and director who graduated from Glasgow University in 1992 and went on to pursue his love of comedy at BBC Scotland. He is best known for co-creating and co-starring in the BAFTA award winning shows *Chewin' the Fat* and *Still Game*. He nearly swam for Canada.

Jules is an actress who trained at the RSAMD. She has worked in theatre, television radio and film for the past thirty years, including on the hit children's show *Balamory*. She is most at home in comedy (at 53, she recently took to the stage for her first ever attempt at stand-up. She was hooked). She is now also a qualified yoga and CWT instructor.

Jules and Greg met on a radio comedy show before starring together in the BBC Scotland comedy *Pulp Video* in 1996. They were married in a hot air balloon in Las Vegas in 1999. They live together with their dog Bonnie by the sea in Fife.

WITH HUGE THANKS TO:

Dawn Steele and Gayle Telfer-Stevens – the OG's; Natalie Valenti, who taught us how to breathe and stretch for life; Tony Kearney and Jim Webster at Solus Productions. With us from the beginning! Rowan Green for sorting everything; Colin and Sean; Captain Kirk, Raonaid; Tom, Richard and Hosh.

The team at BBC Scotland; the viewers who took the time to watch; Sharz for making us look presentable; everyone who swam with us and continues to swim with us.

Sally Reid for our splinter lido aqua group; the Dollan Baths, East Kilbride; Fairview Pool, Dollard-Des-Ormeaux, Montreal; Esther Williams, Johnny Weissmuller and Ron Ely. Special thanks to Ricky Ross and Lorraine McIntosh for introducing us to Tony and for always cheering us on.

The sisters Jo, Sue and Sarah and the brothers, Tony and Steve; Michelle Mcmanus; people of Elie, especially, Judith Dunlop @elieseasidesauna Kay, David and David, Ian and Cath, Jenny and Neil; Laura at Harbour House, The amazing team at G.H Barnett for our Sair Heid chittery bites and of course the Namaste Nips; thanks to Yas Team and all the peri and menopausal women. Keep going, it gets better, we promise! Dondo for being Jules' BP; Laura Doll Doll Doll for all the swim support.

The people at Sea Shell and Heid clothing. The Horror Night Boys (Rab and Paul for trying it and Noddy for continually dinghying it. "It's no for me, lads.")

Self Esteem and the Beach Boys, our favourite music to help us into our cold water tub.

To all the bands who have inspired us (and let us use their music in our show!)

To Jules' papa Benny; our lads, Benny and Chevy, for letting us drag them into the water here, there and everywhere.

Our kid Clarky and Jo.

And Bonnie x

IMAGE CREDITS

All images courtesy of the authors, except those on the following pages © Solus Productions Ltd: viii, 5-6, 9-12, 13-15, 19-23, 28-32, 38, 39-53, 57-60, 64, 70-76, 78, 82, 87-96, 100-101, 104-108, 112-113, 115-120, 122, 126, 129-130, 132, 141, 142 (left)-144, 151 (top), 156, 158, 159 (bottom), 163-173, 175 (top)-183, 193, 196-204, 207-214, 215, 217, 222, 224 (top), 228. Illustrations © Shutterstock.

the *Air Bud* films.) We explained that ours wouldn't talk, or play basketball, but that didn't put him off one bit, and we welcomed eight-week-old Bonnie into the family in May 2015.

It was a no-brainer for Jules that Bonnie would come on this swimming adventure with us. Our cameraman Sean fell in love with her on the very first day of shooting. Now we joke that Bonnie gets more close-ups than we do. But, seriously, we love to see the programme contributors cuddling and making a fuss of her. In many ways, she is acting as a comfort dog, and she's there for anyone who might be nervous before they go on camera. Bonnie is a major part of the team and we really did miss her when we were off filming the rest of series two.

Just like the water, Bonnie is a gentle soul who helps to calm you down. She always waits at the water's edge for us to come back safe. We've noticed in the last wee while since we've moved to the coast that Bonnie's swimming abilities are on the up and up. Jules has bought her a life jacket for series three. Watch this space for that fashion-forward swimming moment! Bonnie has helped bridge the gap, too, since we became empty nesters. It's lovely to hear her pottering round the house, especially on days when you feel a bit down; she's always the perfect excuse to get out and about or go for a drive and a swim. Bonnie only has one true demand. That she gets to go with you. She doesn't like being left behind; it's adorable how seriously she takes her role of being by our side, always! Look, here she is, right now, as we write this chapter about her.

OUTTAKES

When we are shooting, we need people to look after Bonnie; in this case, the lovely Niamh. If you've watched the show, you know Bonnie can be a bit of a diva (she gets bored going in and out of the van), and finding a nice walk for her can be difficult. Sometimes Bonnie hates being separated from us. For example, when we do "up and pasts" in the van. These are the driving shots, where we drive past Sean our cameraman, or shots where Kirk follows us with his drone. All of this footage makes the show look rich and beautiful but, just for the record, Bonnie hates these bits!

JULES & GREG'S WILD SWIM

We might have come to the end, but still we knew a chapter on Bonnie, however short, was essential. Basically because she insisted upon it. For many, she is the star of *Jules & Greg's Wild Swim*, and it makes us laugh how many wonderful people now know her name and love to say hello to her when we are out on a walk.

You will remember in series one how our dog let everyone know who's boss and refused to enter the van without being lifted. This led to a reduced role in series two, but we are currently in talks with her TV agent (a bulldog called Rosie who has an office on Wardour Street) to bring Bonnie back for series three. Only kidding – she couldn't travel with us in series two owing to restrictions on the various ferries to and from the islands.

Before Bonnie, we had a dog called Tootsie for sixteen years. An ace wee mongrel from Cardonald cat and dog home, who we got before we were married. After she passed, Jules said she would never have another dog. But our kids pestered us (particularly the younger one) for a golden retriever. (He was obsessed with

BONUS CHAPTER BONNIE SCOTLAND

Now that I have intermediate knowledge, I've recently kicked it up a few levels with the purchase of a couple of books about, you guessed it, tides. I also recommend Tristan Gooley's enthralling book *How to Read Water*; this phenomenal, eye-opening work is filled with the most amazing, detailed explanations as to why different bodies of water behave the way they do. A must read, if you are curious about cold water dipping.

Why am I telling you all this? In truth, it's because there are so many bodies of water in the UK that are affected by the tides: obviously our coastal waters, but also tidal lochs, bays, estuaries and rivers too. I remember feeling firsthand the dramatic effect of the tide when we swam with the Dundee Dookers and I was being pulled in the opposite direction to the flow of the water. So strange! All this understanding and awareness helps familiarise you with a given regular swim spot. What might be a safe spot at high tide might become more problematic for you at low tide, with exposed rocks, seaweed and so on. Also, water moves differently at high and low tide (more slowly) than it does when it is on the "ebb" and "flood" (more quickly). I will always be curious about the tides. I love them, and from a practical point of view, when it comes to cold water dipping, we equate knowledge, tidal or otherwise, with safety; whereas from a romantic point of view, the tides are where our marine world and our cosmos intersect. So you see, I don't have to choose between my love of Thor Heyerdahl and his hand-built twentieth-century vessel *Kon Tiki* and my adoration for James T. Kirk and his Starship Enterprise.

EMERGENCY NUMBERS

Forgive us for repeating – aka banging on about – this, but there's no fun without safety first . . . so make sure you know your emergency numbers and have them immediately to hand if you or someone else ever get into difficulty.

Emergency numbers: 999 (UK) or 112 (UK & International)
Ask for the Coastguard!

JULES & GREG'S WILD SWIM

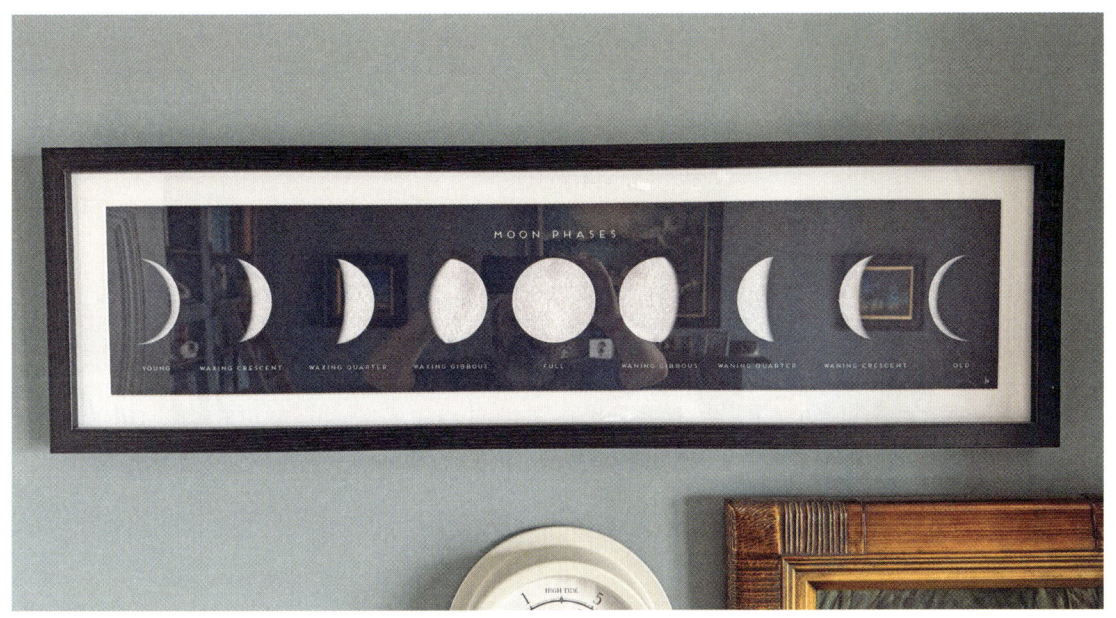

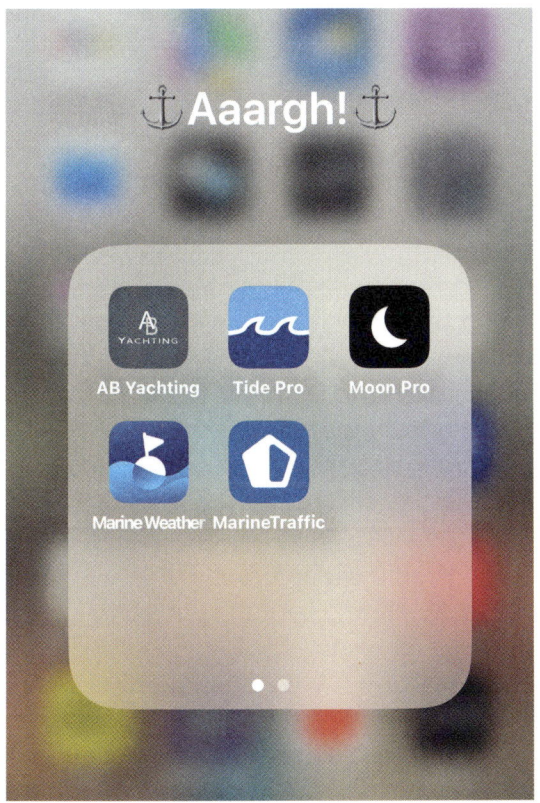

and everything in between. Then I bought a second tidal clock. (A little more sophisticated, more moving parts, more things on its face for me to bore people with.) Then I bought a moon chart. If I know what shape the moon is in the sky, I can work out how many days it is until the next spring tide. Then I bought a tidal chart. I love the fact that thanks to the regular movement of the sun and the moon, sailors can accurately tell us what the tide will be doing in the year 2135. There is something reassuring about this endless constant. Then I downloaded a pro Tide and Moon app for my phone. I can't tell you how many hours I have spent staring out my window watching the tide roll in. Or heading down to the beach to take a closer look at the water advancing through the hundreds of ridges formed in the sand in its silent and inevitable approach. I like to stand rooted on the sand and watch as the water snakes round my feet. Like a Canadian King Knut. (I refuse to spell King Knut with a "C"; it will simply read as if I have dealt myself a horrible moniker.)

Here's a curious thing. The tide advancing seems more exciting than the tide retreating. Why? Maybe it's akin to the feeling you have before a party compared with after. Or why I prefer spring to autumn. Summer is in front of you, not behind. Friday night is better than Saturday night because the weekend is yet to happen. The promise of it thrills. Anticipation is a beautiful thing.

This one looked interesting. I didn't know if it was a true story or a made-up one, and I didn't care. I just wanted to know if the two sailors on the cover survived, and I figured I would find out if I dived in. What a book. It stirred my imagination like a whirlpool and I'm still the proud owner of that very copy. I seemed more interested in naval exploration than space exploration as a child, and I don't really know why. I suppose naval exploration is like the OG analogue version of space exploration to me, so it feels more romantic. (Although I'll argue the case with all comers that the original *Star Trek* TV series is The Greatest TV Show of all Time™.)

So fast forward to 2015, which is when we first started coming to Elie regularly. I had observed (for the first time in my life) that high tide wasn't at the same time each day and also didn't seem to reach the same level on the pier each time. The first observation was simply me being stupid and not knowing the basics: the tide completes on a cycle of twelve hours and twenty-five minutes. So that pesky, uneven extra twenty-five minutes meant that each next high tide was slightly later in the day than the previous one. (Of course, if it took the tide exactly twelve hours to complete its cycle, high and low tide would be at the same time every day, for infinity.)

The latter part, the variance in high tide height, appeared a little more complicated. This, a local explained, was due to the gravitational pull of the moon and (to a lesser extent) the sun. This is when I learned about spring tides and neap tides. A spring tide has nothing to do with the season. It's a description of the

tide "springing forth", and a neap tide is nothing to do with turnips either. Neap is an old English word meaning "scanty" or "without power". When the sun and moon are opposite each other (at the new and full moon) the high tide (and low tide) is more extreme, owing to a greater gravitational pull on our oceans. This is known as a spring tide. When the sun and the moon are less diametrically opposed, sitting "quarterly" in relation to the earth, the gravitational pull of these celestial bodies on the earth's oceans is less extreme, resulting in less impressive tidal heights, known as the scanty "neap" tides.

Well, that was me off. I bought a tidal clock. It tells regular time, but it also has a hand pointing to the high and low tides

GREG'S TIDE CHAT

What a strange thing to become obsessed with at the age of fifty. The tides. But that's exactly what happened.

I tried to trace my fascination with the seas and the ocean back through my life and I think it might have been sparked by an old book on my parents' bookshelf when I was still in single digits. It had a worn-out cover of two sailors braving a ferocious storm on what looked like a raft: *The Kon-Tiki Expedition* by Norwegian adventurer Thor Heyerdahl. I used to sit and stare at that cover. "Why don't you read it?" my mum asked. The only book I remember reading before this one was *Charlotte's Web*, which I had read about three or four times the previous summer.

215

10
GREG'S
TIDE CHAT

THE SEA

And now for some sea safety tips.

1 Check tidal charts at all times. The water outside our house can vary in depth from one metre to over two metres, depending on the type of high tide. It's important to know if you can touch the bottom, especially if you are with less confident or inexperienced swimmers. I know we are stating the obvious here, but better to be safe than sorry!

2 Use those eyeballs to observe what the sea is doing. Wind and breezy gusts turn the sea choppy. Don't like the look of it? Give it a miss till things calm down and instead sit and write a poem about how the sea can be a cruel mistress whose anger will lash and whip you into submission!

3 In the summer months, keep a keen eye out for jellyfish. Red and blue ones aren't too bad, but as we've mentioned that nasty lion's mane jellyfish can pack quite a sting. Be careful!

4 Shoes are essential for many reasons, but we've heard stories of folk getting stung underfoot by weever fish. They burrow under the sand and, unsurprisingly, they do not like to be stood on. Rubber-soled sea shoes will protect you from this rare but unpleasant occurrence.

5 We'll say it again . . . a tow float is essential for sea swimming. There are many people using the water who NEED to

see you. Paddleboarders, sailboats, power boaters, jet-skiers, windsurfers.

6 If you are worried about swimming in the sea, then a tidal pool can be a great option. They are a much more controlled environment, protecting you from many of the elements of sea swimming, but still giving you an uplifting outdoor sea and salt experience!

7 If you find yourself struggling in the water, the RNLI suggest you should 'float to live'. They hae a song written for kids, but is applicable to us all, 'If you get in trouble, just float like this / Use your arms and legs like a big starfish.'

WATERFALLS

> **SWIM SPOT**
>
> ### LEALT FALLS
>
> The Lealt Falls on the Isle of Skye was our first stop when we visited the island. Jules had swum in a waterfall before, but I hadn't. There are many safety protocols that should be observed when swimming in such conditions, and it's also handy to have a local person who knows exactly what they are doing. One such was Matt, our guide on the island, who did a risk assessment before we entered, for which we were grateful because waterfalls have many changeable hazards that you can't really see with the naked eye. Hidden boulders, shifting currents, whitewater churned by the falling water. We recommend doing as much research as possible on any body of water like this. Safety knowledge is vital!
>
>

STAR SWIMMERS
THE FREEZING FANNIES

Jules announced that we were on our way to meet the Frozen Fannies. Right. (As it turns out, they are actually called the Freezing Fannies . . .) This swim was an unusual one. We stood there looking down on this fast-flowing, dark and deep river and, while I felt okay with it, Jules seemed genuinely nervous. I reassured her that we were going in with a group of locals who know the river well. We ended up having one of our favourite swims so far in a river that turned out to be very inviting. We swam up it and floated back. You don't see it on camera, but Jules spotted a deer drinking from the river as we were swimming upstream. She likes to call it her *Stand by Me* moment. "You wouldn't see that at the Dollan Baths, would ye?" she quipped.

The Fannies were full of tips on how and when to enter a river safely. They had a goggle-wearing spotter who would take a quick look to make sure there was no hidden or dangerous obstacles beneath the water. Rivers are different from other bodies of water in that what lies beneath the surface can change dramatically if there has been a storm or heavy rainfall. As Jules says, "This is why I find my back yard tub so useful. I don't like swimming in open water after a downpour!"

Colleen swims with this group and she deserves special mention. She was inducted into the Marathon Hall of Swimming Fame in New York City for her numerous, incredible open-water achievements, including a Channel swim and crossing the Minch between the Scottish mainland and Lewis. She is a ferociously capable swimmer, and off camera she took Greg into the main current and showed him how she trains. Basically, she swims on the spot as she fights the current which travels in the opposite direction. Greg was absolutely rubbed after only a few minutes though Colleen will train in this manner for forty-five minutes at a time. The group's motto is "Swim for Strength, Endurance and Stamina". Colleen and her pals certainly have all three in abundance.

RIVERS

If you are nervous about river swimming, you are right to be. We would recommend you follow the advice we were given. First and foremost, do not do it alone. Join a local group who know the body of water really well, and listen to their tips to ensure a safe and enjoyable swim. Watch out for how to spot the strength and flow of the river, the pull of the currents, when it's safe to swim and not; for example, heavy rainfall or a storm can affect the speed of river flow for many days afterwards, and this must be taken into consideration. Know your entry and exit points, so that you are getting out near your kit. The most experienced swimmers advise swimming upstream and then enjoying the relaxation of letting the flow of the river carry you back to your kit. We learned about the "ferry glide", which is the safe way of removing yourself from a current. Basically, you give yourself over to the current by not fighting it and so swim gently towards the side or the riverbank. Greg was so excited to learn this new swimming term that he slips it into conversation whenever he can...

KNOW YOUR BODIES OF WATER: LOCHS, RIVERS, WATERFALLS AND SEAS

LOCHS

There are an estimated 30,000 lochs in Scotland. Never mind Munro bagging, try loch bagging!

SWIM SPOT

LOCH NESS

We were excited for our next swim location on Loch Ness at Dores Beach because this is where it all began for us. It was thanks to this beach a few years previously that Jules had the idea for the show. We were driving back to Glasgow, and she pondered how wonderful it would be to front a swimming show and talk to as many people as we could about their reasons for doing wild swimming. It was a lovely and strange feeling to return to that spot with our crew, ready to dive in and meet another swim group. Loch Ness, for obvious reasons, is a storied spot, but one of the things that always strikes us most is the sense you get of its phenomenal depth. Mere metres from the shoreline and you can no longer touch the bottom. At 37 kilometres long and 230 metres deep, it's an ancient water-filled ravine running south of Inverness. Loch Ness is unusual in that it takes a long time to heat up and a long time to cool down, making it the coldest loch to swim in in the summer and the warmest loch to swim in in the winter.

BEFORE YOU DIVE IN

WEATHER CONDITIONS

Here are some tips about what to look out for weather wise when deciding to go for a dip.

- See our advice about swimming in rivers immediately after heavy rainfall. It's worth saying again. Don't do this.

- Your best barometer is your eyeballs. We check many weather and wind apps before we go, but a visual read is as good as anything. We've often cancelled swims if we arrive at a loch and don't fancy the look of the whitecaps. Trust your instinct on this one.

- Wind is a consideration when entering water. Emerging from your swim into a cold and blasting wind can be not only unpleasant but also downright challenging, so take care. If in doubt avoid or wait for the wind to die down. OR be ready to jump quickly into your warms (or a nearby café or car) when you emerge from the water.

- Offshore winds are the ones to be wary of. These are the winds that come from onshore and head out to sea. We have on many occasions felt the push of an offshore wind gently ebbing us away from the shore. Genuinely, this can be very scary. If you feel the wind pushing you out, best to get out the water sharpish.

- ALWAYS cover your dry kit before you go into the water. You will need it to remain dry for when you come out. Many times we have gone in on a clear sky ("Don't worry!" we chirp. "Hardly any clouds. Our clothes will be fine!"), only for black clouds to appear out of nowhere and soak our pile of dry clothes sitting on the beach.

- Sunshine can pose a problem by creating a false sense of security. March is the coldest time of year for sea water in Scotland. But days can feel very warm and sunny in March, and so the water takes on a much more inviting appearance . . . but in reality, it can be absolutely perishing. We therefore recommend caution when entering March waters on a sunny day.

IMPORTANT RESOURCES

For more info on swimming safety, check out:
www.rnli.org/safety
www.outdoorswimmingsociety.com

BEFORE YOU DIVE IN

1 **Buy and always wear water shoes.** They will give you confidence and protect your feet.

2 **Buy a tow float.** Essential for visibility if you are swimming near boats, etc.

3 **Always tell someone your location if going swimming.** This is vital even if you are in company, not just when you are alone.

4 **Avoid jumping in.** It can give you a nasty shock. We like to ease ourselves in. Always remember you may not know exactly what is beneath the water; there could be rocks, broken branches, etc.

5 **Always research your swimming spot.** Take the time to read about where you are headed. There's a good chance there'll be plenty of information online from swimmers who have been before you.

6 **Always take loose layers** to put on after your dip.

7 **And, please, always get your wets off** as soon as possible.

8 **Bring a hot drink.** Anything that helps to warm you up speedily after your dip.

9 **Time yourself.** Remember, you only need to be in the water for thirty seconds to three minutes for cold water therapy to work its magic.

10 **Avoid rivers after storms for at least two days.** You will notice much faster flowing water at these times and that is not conducive to a pleasant or safe dip.

11 **You might like to avoid the sea after heavy rainfall too.** We don't like going in when it is too murky. Murkiness in the summer can mask that dreaded enemy of the wild swimmer, the lion's mane jellyfish!

12 **Putting your head underwater is not mandatory when cold water dipping**, though plenty of folk love to do it. If you must, we recommend doing it in company not when you are on your own as sometimes dizziness can occur.

13 **If you are not a confident swimmer, always stay within your depth:** that means feet on the ground in water without a current.

14 **Invest in a pair of water earplugs.** This can help you to swim longer as they protect your ears from water and can also protect against light-headedness.

This is just for starters. Look online for more safety tips; you really cannot read enough about this vital element of wild swimming. You will build up your own safety routine over time. Go with what works best for you!

SWIMMING IN GROUPS

LISTEN TO EXPERTS

We have learned so much from the experts we have spoken to on our show so far. We learned great safety tips about breaking loch ice from Alice Goodridge, invaluable advice on currents and river swimming from Colleen Blair and the Frozen Fannies of Aberfeldy (we will never forget how to ferry glide), and Anna Deacon and Vicky Allan's wild swimming books cover so many safety aspects that we still take our copy of *The Art of Wild Swimming: Scotland* with us when going for a new swim. And we still employ Natalie Valenti's breathing techniques when entering the water on a particularly cold day.

We urge you to make your own approach to water safety as thorough as can be. In the meantime, here is our by-no-means-exhaustive list of fourteen safety points.

are designed to get wet. In winter Jules doesn't really dunk her head, whereas I feel I've cheated myself if I don't. A neoprene hat offers much-needed protection from brain freeze or "ice cream head" (as we are often heard shouting in the show), so I can dip my head and not get that dizzy feeling. There are plenty who are of the opinion that there is no benefit to dipping your head, especially in winter. But I like to do it, as I always feel better and more refreshed than if I don't. So, these hats are excellent if you wish to dook your head, but other safety tips include starting with short, quick head dips, staying in shallow water with your feet on the ground and only doing it when in the company of other swimmers, who can help if you do get that dizzy feeling. Again, go with your gut. But always, safety first.

Portable Radio

This little device comes highly recommended by Jules. On a nice day, especially sitting round a fire, it creates an instant, easy beach party ambience and helps break the ice if swimmers are unfamiliar with each other. If you are young, like our sons, then you can jump straight to a Bluetooth speaker and set a swimming playlist on your phone. Please of course be mindful of others around you and avoid disturbing them with too much noise.

Incense

Jules is incense daft. She believes incense makes a nice little addition to your kit, but remember, here in the UK it can be difficult to light outdoors in those winter months. Incense is especially nice to set up before your swim as it helps calm people and encourages gentle breathing on exiting that cold water. It's all part of grounding yourself and being outside in nature.

Nordic Socks

What can we say about this post-dip essential apart from: "Buy them right now. What are you doing buying only one pair, are you crazy? You need at least three, four or five pairs." These Nordic beauties, within a very short space of time, will become your best pals and the only socks in your winter swim wardrobe.

Sleeved Swimming Suits

To sleeve or not to sleeve? Jules has a few of these suits in her basket for winter swims and, to be honest, this one's up to you and the level of comfort versus discomfort you want to subject yourself to when you dip. There is no right and wrong; it's a matter of personal preference. The same goes for wetsuits. Some folk like to wear a full winter wetsuit and stay in the water for a good length of time, or they'll opt for a summer one (short sleeves and short legs) to offer a little comfort while they dip. I prefer no wetsuit because when it comes to dipping, a wetsuit feels like the equivalent of wearing your winter coat indoors. I want that cold water against my skin. The trade-off, however, is that, midwinter, I rarely stay in the water for more than three minutes. As soon as that alarm hits, I am OUT. I should also point out, within the first five years of coming to Fife, the idea of entering the water without some form of wetsuit never occurred to me. It was simply a nonstarter. I've now shed those protective layers, but it took time just to get my head around the idea. So don't let anyone tell you what you should or shouldn't do. When it comes to swimming suits and wetsuits, best to suit yourself.

Swimming Hats

Specifically, the neoprene ones. Not a great idea to ruin your woolly hat by going underwater with it, but the neoprene ones

of euphoria as I made my way back to the intense heat of the sauna. Michael was putting no pressure on himself to enter the water; he wasn't sure he was going to go through with it, but like a trooper, he did. Multiple times. He seemed to get a real kick out of it, and I felt equally happy for him that he'd got to have that experience.

Wylding Boiler Suit
Jules owns two of these fleece-lined, all-in-one beauties and she swears by them for coming out of the water. When she is teaching yoga on a cold and windy beach, this suit is her go-to. I think she looks a bit like Michael Myers in John Carpenter's *Halloween* and I'll often whistle the theme tune as she comes down the stairs in her Wylding. She cares not a jot. She has thick skin in this regard and never takes offence. I think she secretly loves the comparison because she's a massive *Halloween* fan herself. Plus, the occasion of Halloween is a big deal in our house: we have one box of Christmas decorations and eight boxes of Halloween decorations.

are so easy to get on. So you come out the water, you are freezing, you strip and you are getting battered by the elements. Socks then shoes can be tricky if not downright difficult when you are standing there and your fingers are numb. But you can get these boots on in seconds, offering instant protection to your extremities and raising your body heat. TLDR: I would 10/10 recommend a pair of these! You will not regret it. Out the water to warm feet in less than fifteen seconds. Boom.

Dryrobe Gloves
So, after all the rhapsodising about the boots, Jules got me a pair of these. But I don't love them. For me, they are too fiddly.

Thermometer
The water temperature range in Scotland moves between roughly 15°C in the summer and 6°C in the winter. That's for our coastal waters. Lochs can get colder still as they warm up and cool down more quickly than ocean water, which is why we will often see ice on the edges of a loch during a cold snap. We rarely bring a thermometer because, come hell or cold water, we are going in, whatever the month. But there is usually someone in the group who likes to use a thermometer – maybe because they are recording their swims in a journal and temperatures between bodies of water can vary, or simply because they like to know. If someone brings a thermometer, my curiosity will always get the better of me and I'll ask the temperature, but sometimes ignorance is bliss. The one constant for me, like so many swimmers and dippers, is that I never ever want to get in the water at the beginning. Even while I'm getting ready, I can feel my mind scanning and searching quietly for reasons not to do it. This is the hardest part of the whole experience for me to overcome. Myself. My brain. A necessary companion obviously but a bit of a shitebag all the same.

The coldest water I have ever swum in was Helsinki with my friend Michael. It was a very memorable experience: the water temperature was 1°C. A temperature of 1°C always makes me smile. It instantly takes me back to one of my favourite lines from one of my favourite comedies, *Planes, Trains and Automobiles*. Steve Martin and John Candy are riding in the back of an open pickup truck midwinter and Martin asks his companion, "What do you think the temperature is?" John Candy answers: "One." It's a little throwaway joke, but it always makes me roar with laughter. For some reason, "one" sounds colder than "zero". We were on a sauna excursion in the home of saunas, a two-hour session where you sat in 80 to 90°C temperatures then plunged into the Gulf of Finland, a body of water south of Helsinki that leads into the Baltic Sea. The water felt as if it was about to turn into slush but wasn't quite there yet. I'm not the type to jump in, and I needed every ounce of discipline to keep calm and exhale as I lowered my shoulders and the back of my neck into the water. We must have entered the water about five or six times over the two hours and it was never harder than the first time. The cold seemed to attack every inch of my body, and I felt numbness and pins and needles everywhere, followed by a sense

Dry Robe/Dock and Bay Towels

Do not get us wrong. Dryrobes are great (we own about five in our family), but they are expensive and many other great gowns/coats have emerged that are a lot more affordable. The cool thing about the original Dryrobe for me was that not only did it keep you incredibly warm, it is in effect a mobile changing room. Great for shy, modest characters like me, who don't want to flash anybody. Not that wild swimmers really give a damn. Everybody is so focused on getting out their wets and getting warm. We are quite a liberal bunch when it comes to that kind of body stuff. It's one of the nice side effects of this community. You stop caring about what you look like and you shed your inhibitions a bit. But aye, a mobile changing room, there you go. What's not to love?

Dryrobe Boots

Okay, these are, for my money, the greatest accessory money can buy. What's so great about them? Well, cold water swimming in the winter can be even more challenging in Scotland than other parts of the UK. Any combination of wind, rain and cold can make for an uncomfortable, even unpleasant winter dip. Let me tell you that the Dryrobe boots are sensational for one reason above all else. They

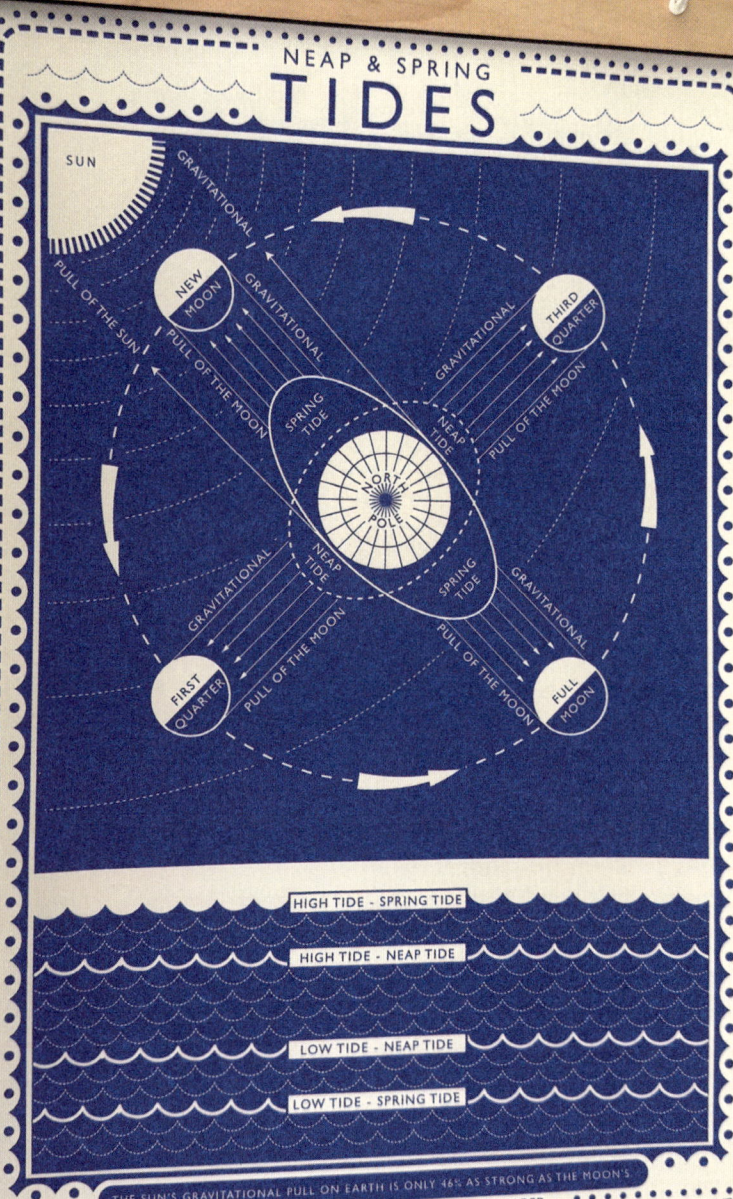

JULES & GREG'S WILD SWIM

Barrel

We got our barrel from Lithuania and it's proved a very worthwhile purchase. Despite living by the sea, there are plenty of days, especially through winter, where heading into the bay is just not advisable. Between the gusts and the swell, the safer option is to climb into your barrel rather than being thrown about on the waves like a cork, thereby ensuring you still get your fix on days when the outdoors isn't playing nice. Now there are barrels that have expensive cold filter kits attached, and the like. These can run up in price to between £4,000 and £6,000. We prefer a more straightforward barrel, and as long as you change the water every few days, you can pick one up for as little as £30 to £100, or if you'd like to splash out on a custom-built one, you can pay a little more, about £1,000. But listen, until you have worked out if you enjoy this madness, do NOT spend a bunch of money. We have pals whose "barrel" is in fact their wheelie bin. (Take the rubbish out, give it a wee clean and you're good to go.)

Moon Bag

What a cool wee thing the moon bag is. You can pick them up for about £30. Jules loves hers! The moon bag is a bag that you stand on to get changed, then when you come out the water, all your wets go in the middle, you pull a drawstring and over your shoulder it goes and you're off. Jules always sings its praises because half the time you can be standing either in a thistly field or on big smooth flat stones, and something to stand on can make all the difference!

THE FUN STUFF

One truly fun thing about this pastime is that as you immerse yourself deeper into it, as your community of lovely likeminded folk expands, you will inevitably find yourself saying these words to a fellow dipper: "What the hell is that wee thing and where can I get one?" Swimmers, like so many sporty hobbyists, love a new bit of clothing or a gadget. And there are plenty of forces out there mad keen to sell them to us.

Again, you don't need the stuff we list here. But if you find yourself falling in love with this new hobby, you might want to treat yourself to a few fun items. These are the ones we use the most.

Snug Buds
The two Emmas:

Emma 1 used to get very cold hands and one day after a swim, she pulled a hot-water bottle over her shoulders and her hands disappeared INSIDE it. Cue us: "Emma, what the hell is that wee thing and where can we get TWO?"

Two days later, we had a pair of Snug Buds™ delivered to our door, and we still take them on every swim.

Fladen Suit
Emma 2 we met in Shetland. A nurse and all-round local legend, Jules had met her and within twenty seconds asked her about her suit. Turns out Emma was kitted out in a Fladen flotation suit. Now these things don't come cheap. (So Jules and I bought them for each other as anniversary gifts to ourselves.) You can see us cutting about the East Neuk when we are walking Bonnie in gale-force weather. We basically look like rescue services or traffic wardens. Sure, we look like we are dressed for life on an oil rig, but you simply cannot slag our attire until you have walked a mile in our suits. Warm and cosy does not begin to cover it.

Thank you, fabulous Emmas, for introducing us to some kit that has improved our swimming (and dog-walking) experience no end!

Fire Pit
A raised portable fire pit can be purchased from any reputable outdoor shop and shouldn't set you back too much. These are handy for keeping your group warm, but please remember to leave any area "as you found it".

JULES'S WOOLLEN HATS

Very quickly in the show, a running joke became apparent. Every time we were near a gift shop, Jules bought not one but two hats. She couldn't help herself. Here she is, defending her hat addiction:

Straight up, a good hat is as important a part of your kit as anything . . . a dry robe, a Nordic sock, the humble woolly hat, all of these let you stay in the water longer. See? Right away, you need two hats. One while you're in the water and another nested in your bag, nice and dry, for when you come out. Because let's face it, the one in the water is going to get wet.

Jules is proud of her ever-growing hat collection and, like all good collectors, she knows exactly where she got each one or exactly who gave her them! Those hats offer another layer of security when you are in that freezing water. She also wears them in the tub through the winter.

And get this: the nickname her sisters gave her when she was three years old is "Wee Woolie Hat". A huge collection of hats was evidently . . . her destiny.

THE ESSENTIALS

Sea Shoes

You can get a good pair for between £10 and £20. They will give you confidence going into any loch or beach without worrying about your bare feet. Lochs can have rocks or debris that has lain there for years and sea shoes give you the "backing" to negotiate these things, reducing the chance of cutting or injuring yourself. If you want to spend a bit more, you can get neoprene boots which will actually keep your feet warmer when in the water too. If you do a lot of coastal or sea swimming, you can expect to be replacing these shoes every year or two. The salty sea water seems to wear particularly hard on your sea shoes. Eventually you will graduate to boots WITH ZIPS. But not yet, grasshopper, not yet. Patience.

Gloves

The thing most people struggle with, particularly in those chilly winter months, is their extremities getting cold. Jules always finds that her toes are the last thing to warm up, so footwear is vital for her, but gloves give her the same protection against baltic conditions. Some people use them all year round; others only require gloves in the winter months. See how you go and work out what is best for you, but we rarely head for a swim without our diver's gloves. They're awesome and they make those three minutes that for us constitute a winter dip that much easier!

Hats

I'm not going to lie to you here; we have a hollowed-out garden chair in our hallway bursting with woolly hats. Do you remember Imelda Marcos and her three thousand pairs of shoes? Jules is the Imelda Marcos of woollen swimming hats. Suffice it to say, these will offer you a bit of heat, comfort and confidence, again, in those winter months. But I'm not going to cover "woollen hats" here. They are going to need their own section.

Tow Float

An essential bit of kit, essential we tell ya! Especially if you are a solo dipper. With a belt you can clip around your waist, you can keep all your affects in your trusty waterproof tow float (car keys, mobile, wallet/purse). It is especially vital in areas where there is any marine traffic, where it is very important to make yourself visible. As it's inflated and buoyant, it's also great to catch a breath on if you are on a longer swim. You will have seen from the show that Jules sometimes uses her tow float as a Graham Norton-style sofa while she interviews someone in the water!

Flask and "Chittery Bite"

Jules never, NEVER EVER leaves for a swim without her trusty flask of tea (and she doesn't even mind if the tea gets stewed beyond the point that a builder would reject it) and a chocolate biscuit of some sort. There are better people than us to tell you the science of a quick glucose injection after a cold swim, but all we can say is: a biscuit (or three) and a cup of tea after some cold-water action is mandatory for us.

SWIM KIT

Whenever you are curious about taking up anything new, the first thing that might cause you to put the brakes on is the question: how much equipment do I need to buy? What are the essentials that I shouldn't attempt this thing without? What stuff do I need? Jules and I always echo the words of the fabulous Anna Deacon, as she has said so often in her many publications: not much, actually. We subscribe to her philosophy, which is to start with a scanty pile of kit and build up to buying the things you find you genuinely need.

For full disclosure, Jules and I have bought a lot of STUFF over the five years we have been cold water swimming. Okay, I've bought a BIT of stuff and Jules has bought a LOT of stuff. She cannot deny it. Barely a day goes by where I am not in receipt of the latest package from Amazon, UPS, DPD and every other organisation that now brings the high street straight to our door. I am on first-name terms with our delivery drivers. We have a LOT of swimming stuff.

But the important point is, we did not START with a lot of swimming stuff. All you need to begin with is a towel and a swimming costume. And if you are in the right company and your beach or swimming spot is remote enough, you don't even need the costume. Just the towel, to get dry. Getting dry quickly is very important in wild swimming, and it's where so much other stuff comes in handy, besides simply towels, but we'll get to that.

> **SWIM TIP**
>
> On Harris, just a few days before we went out for a sea swim on a windy day, the RNLI had to rescue a kayaker in an inflatable because they had been pushed out by the very same offshore wind we were about to swim in. Safety tip: Inflatables and offshore winds are not a good mix. If in doubt about wind direction, check with someone who knows better before you find yourself clinging for dear life to that inflatable doughnut...

THE BEST TIME TO GO SWIMMING

It's worth bearing in mind that if you have anxiety about entering cold water, but are nevertheless keen to start wild swimming, then August and September are the best months for you to do so. Basically, temperature wise, this is as good as it gets! Our island adventure was filmed in August 2024 when Scotland was being battered by some of the worst weather ever seen. It's on record as one of the wettest summers ever. We mention this because taking the weather into account, as well as water temperature, is absolutely vital for wild swimmers. We say it again for those at the back: it's not JUST the water you must brave; it's the elements before and after your dip. In Scotland, you can go to the exact same spot twice on the same day of the year and have two completely different experiences because of the weather. So knowing this, please make sure you get kitted up. (Jules loves this bit. She buys kit all the time.)

We'll talk later about the kit you need, but the basics are:

1. Loose clothing for layering up

2. Towels, to get dry THE MINUTE you exit the water

3. Water shoes (buy off the internet for fifteen quid) to give you confidence in unknown bodies of water

4. Gloves to protect the extremities if your hands tend to get cold

5. A long, warm waterproof jacket with a hood. (We love our branded Dryrobes, but there are many different types now available. Shop around.) You will not regret buying this when you are getting changed in the wind and the rain. A good waterproof robe is basically a mobile changing room. Here in Scotland, where extreme weather is so prevalent and so changeable, it is a vital resource to keep you comfortable.

THE DOS AND DON'TS OF WILD AND COLD WATER SWIMMING

There's no fun without safety. It's really important that we tell you about how to keep yourself safe while swimming – and that you listen carefully! We want you to keep swimming for longer.

Our son is named after Jules's papa Benny, who sadly drowned at age sixty in Whitley Bay on a family holiday after trying to reach his daughter (Joan, Jules's mum), who had been pulled out to sea by the currents. Jules, who was three at the time, remembers it vividly. She was there with her sisters, and these events remain an impossibly difficult chapter in her family's story. After Benny Sr died, Joan sent all four daughters to East Kilbride Dollan Baths for swimming lessons. We mention this because whenever we set foot in any body of water, for Jules there is always an extra element of caution. As a mum and a person who wild swims on the TV, she feels acutely her responsibility to highlight the risks and dangers as well as the joys of open-water dipping and swimming.

Safety first, always. It is vital to give the sea the respect it deserves.

SWIM TIP

BEWARE THE WIND

While we were out swimming with a local group on Harris for the show, we realised just how strong and potent the current and wind can be as a combined force. While Jules was talking to one of the swimmers, Mhairi, the two of them were pushed a hundred yards out in a matter of moments. Jules was literally interviewing Mhairi in the water and the two of them, along with cameraman Sean, were floating away. I had to shout at them both to start making their way back in, and being strong swimmers, they did so easily.

9
BEFORE YOU DIVE IN

Is it strange that we simply don't want this experience to end? If anything, it feels as if we are just at the start of things. The minute we finish, after a couple of days' rest, we are ready to set off on our next adventure. Where are we going next? The Borders? Ayrshire? Yorkshire? Ireland? Wales? Norway? Canada? There's a lot of water out there, an infinite amount really, and a thriving and growing wild swimming community whose stories we are eager to hear. We honestly can't thank all of our contributors enough. Our show was never really about the places, beautiful and mind-blowing as they are; it was always about the beautiful and mind-blowing people who swim in them. We thank them all so much for sharing their precious time and being so open and honest with us. We know for a fact that each of your stories has encouraged so many people to give this wild swimming lark a go and take their first steps into the water.

We know because they tell us every day. So, thank you from the bottom of our hearts to each and every one of you.

It really does feel as if we have made new friends for life!

tides throwing us fiercely about were not without their challenges. We definitely swallowed more than our fair share of sea water on this series, but we also definitely learned that we are both tougher and stronger than we ever thought. When people talk to us about this show, they tell us they'd love to try wild swimming, but they are not as brave as us. We are here to tell you that you are. All you need is a little encouragement, a little support and, dare we say it, a little nudge across the beach and into the sea.

We don't like to waste time wishing we had started ten years earlier and neither should you. If you are curious and almost ready to give it a go, don't put it off any longer. If we've learned one thing, there's no bad time to start. If you start in the summer, you can chart the gradual falling-off of temperature as you head into winter and you won't find it so shocking. If you start in the winter, then you know you can swim at any time of year after that! So, it's win-win. Swim swim!

Since we started this adventure, we have swum in places we never imagined we would get to, including Orkney and Shetland, the Outer Hebrides, Glencoe, Dublin, Oslo and Helsinki. We have plans to go to Canada, Wales, England and hopefully one day St Kilda. Watch this space! If you spot us, then come say hello and feel free to join us for a swim.

STAR SWIMMER
THE SEAFIELD SINKERS

Lara from the Seafield Sinkers in the East Neuk of Fife spoke eloquently about her love of wild swimming and the community she's part of. She loves the fact that it's such a relaxed space for folk to come together and open up to one another about anything they might be going through. Her connection to her fellow swimmers was worn on her dry robe in the form of a mosaic of swimming badges she had collected over time spent with so many groups. Jules loved it so much she decided to copy her and now her dry robe, too, resembles a biker's jacket with its multiple patches of all the cool people she's swum with.

If you are in any way curious about this whole escapade, Jules is adamant you join a swimming group.

Let them look after you. Let them coax you in, warm you up, make pals with you, get you addicted to the joy of wild waters. Let them make you laugh, let them dry your tears, let them surprise you. Let them teach you about the moon and the tides, let them bring out the hippie side of you. To join a swimming group is simply to co-opt a whole new bunch of pals you didn't know you needed in your life. And remember, you are never ever too old to make new pals. (Greg's mum Anne taught us this.)

We finished our island adventure with a party on the beach, with some of Shetland's very best musicians. It was a great party but also an emotional end to a long month's filming.

We had begun this trip a month earlier in a state of anxiety. Would our kids be okay while we were away? Would they remember to feed Bonnie? Would it be as enjoyable as the first time round? Or was it going to be too tough for us? It certainly was tough; those Atlantic swims with the wind, gusts, currents, waves and

8
JUMP IN – THE WATER'S GREAT

SWIM SPOT

LUSKENTYRE BEACH

Our next stop was Luskentyre Beach. The landscape on Harris is breathtaking, with its high inclines, dramatic glens and colossal, sublime rock formations. But this beach is ridiculous. That's the best we can do. We can't think of any other word that describes it better. Ridiculous. Luskentyre is world famous and gets a mention in pretty much every travel book published about Scotland. Pure white sands stretching for miles and blending with beautifully desolate, empty dunes, Luskentyre easily earns its regular inclusion in those lists of the world's top ten beaches.

The irony is that we never swam there, as we had completed our swimming for that filming day already, but we know full well there is no way we are not going back to this beach. The minute we left, we began talking about how and when we were going to get back to it. It's always incredible (and comical) to us how good the crew are at finding hiding spots in these vast open spaces; we have wonderful photos of them peeking out of long grass, hiding in boats and any unsuspecting spot they can find. They are expert hide-and-seekers, but more importantly, we have to open up on camera in front of them, and they are a wonderfully supportive and understanding bunch of crew. Jules gets nervous about filming these sequences because she never knows what's going to come out of her mouth. But that's because she is so relaxed in the company of our crew and totally trusts them. Whenever we do a job in television, we realise how easy it is to get close to your crew. The hours are long, you're often up close together in tiny rooms, but with a smaller crew on a show such as *Jules & Greg's Wild Swim*, you become bonded as a surrogate family that does everything together. It makes for a wonderful experience. The crew are so talented at what they do, they ARE a wee family to us; most of them have been with us since the pilot. Sean, our cameraman, Kirk our drone operator, Colin on sound, Rowan who does everything, Jim our producer, our amazing editors Thom, Richard, Claire and Hosh, and Tony our all-round superb director. This small band of pirates is our crew/family and we love setting off on our adventures with them.

THE MAGIC CURE – COMMUNITY

LUKE THE DUKE

A moment of silence, please, for our fantastic camper van, Luke the Duke.

Poor Luke – we really put him through his paces. From Fife to the Outer Hebrides, Luke was our faithful mode of transportation. Many a time we thought, this is it, Luke has driven his last mile. And still, miracle of miracles, he persisted! In Harris, when it really did come to pass that the end was in sight for our home on wheels, a lovely mechanic called George was summoned to take him away in a grimly painful ceremony.

We never saw Luke the Duke again, but that van is often in our thoughts. What, you might ask, happens in a TV show when the on-screen transport dies? The fun and games begin. Our producer Jim starts a series of phone calls up and down the Hebrides in search of a replacement van. In the meantime, we jump in with the rest of the crew and head off regardless. Eventually, word reaches us that someone in Lewis has lent us a van. It's a school bus and they have kindly donated it to us. They have saved the day. We're back on the road, but God knows how those poor kids got to school.

SWIMMING PLAYLIST

'INTO THE OCEAN'
BLUE OCTOBER

GREG

Jules and I both hail from places where people leave when they hit a certain age. In most cases, this exodus was driven by necessity. Whether it was to go make their mark on the world, start or further a career, or simply to broaden their horizons. But in today's age of unparalleled tech and communication, we seem to be seeing a massive shift, a sea change in the younger generation, who no longer feel the need to pack up, leave their families and sweat it in a tiny bedsit in London. (Such bedsits, if they still exist, being frankly unaffordable.) Perhaps, I think, the greatest gift the internet will give us is that of not removing youngsters from the place they grew up, from everything they know, but instead encouraging them to build their lives on a really strong base, surrounded by loved ones who will nurture and support them in their vision, right on the doorsteps of the places they call home.

We count ourselves among this movement. We can live in a fishing village with a population of 250 people and write every day. (As long as our Wi-Fi holds up.) Most actors we know have at some point uprooted and headed to London; it was drilled into us that if we were serious about making a success of an acting career, we needed to head to the metropolis. Most such actors we know have now returned home, having realised this was what could politely be described as bollocks. The younger generation are smarter than us. What took us twenty years, they realised in two minutes. In short, those young folk who build something for themselves at home are to be envied and admired (them and their tiny carbon footprint).

THE BOOKSHELF

THE OUTRUN BY AMY LIPTROT

check with your doctor if you are concerned about swimming while pregnant, especially if that swimming is "wild", but it was nice to hear yet another benefit to add to the list of why we should get in the water.

I wish I had swum while pregnant, instead of eating ginger nut biscuits, pineapple cakes and guzzling Gaviscon by the gallon.

This swim was another example of a time when we really didn't want to go in but were so glad we did by the time we came out. (This is surely the first rule of any sport you love: it's tough to get out there and do it – whether it's a run, a yoga session, fitness class or swim – but you *always* feel better afterwards.) This one was an exhilarating swim, the type our cameraman Sean loves. He gets in among us, howling with laughter, and he has an amazing knack for shoving a camera into our faces just in time to see us getting slapped by a wave. I don't wish to discuss the fact that my full arse is on display during this swim. The less said about that the better. (For those of a strong disposition, you can freeze-frame at 25:17).

We don't normally mix booze with swimming, but we made an exception in this case. It was a pleasure to sit looking out at the North Atlantic and sample the products of Johnny and Kate's labour, in a bespoke van kitted out by their lovely pal Rob. Another young man who has returned to make customised vans on Benbecula his business. Very cool.

simply places that young people left. It is interesting in the modern day to see a new trend emerging; here is a generation that's now eschewing the big cities and instead are focused on growing thriving small businesses once more in the rural areas they came from.

Johnny and Kate make gin all day and go swimming on their lunch break. It's hard not to think they're winning at life with a routine like that. Their gin is called Downpour. Incidentally, it won't surprise you to know that we gave it a try and it really was sensational. No contest if we were to choose between Downpour and a big supermarket brand – plus, as Jules says, the bottles are far nicer.

JULES

I was a little apprehensive of this swim. The swell was quite large and there seemed to be a significant pull from a current. Our cameraman Sean gave an excellent briefing on how to stay safe in such conditions. We had to wear our tow floats for visibility and for if we got tired, and we had to stay relatively shallow. Kate assured us that we were in safe hands. The boys surfed these waters every day, and in the end we took to the wild swell with confidence. Kate told me that when she was pregnant and struggling with morning sickness, the only thing that would placate it was a swim in the sea. Of course you should always

THE MAGIC CURE – COMMUNITY

THE KIDS ARE COMING HOME

On Benbecula, at a place called Cula Bay, we are all set to meet a young couple, Johnny and Kate, who have returned home, settled down with their baby and opened a whisky and gin distillery. While they await the maturation of their whisky, they are making gin. Their USP is to use local botanicals from the surrounding area. It's refreshing to be in the company of younger folk who have taken their entrepreneurial spirit and retuned home with it, to allow the place they grew up in to reap the benefits of their energy and ideas. For many generations all across Scotland, rural communities were once

STAR SWIMMER
ANNA DEACON AND THE WARDIE BAY SWIMMERS

Anna started swimming down at Wardie Bay just along the coast from Leith, Edinburgh. She used to walk her dog and notice the odd swimmer, so she put out a social media post to see if anyone wanted to dip with her. Fast forward ten years and she and Vicky Allan have created multiple books about cold water swimming detailing groups and locations not just in Scotland, but all over the UK, Ireland and Spain.

Wardie Bay is a residential area with newbuild flats, old fishermen's cottages and a road busy with buses and lorries; it's next to a harbour and is a perfect example of an accessible urban swim spot. Right in the midst of the city, looking across to Fife, the Firth of Forth feels like a vast open space to swim, but we felt safe with Anna and her group. For us, this felt better than any gym membership. These women talked of always doing this. They can't imagine stopping. "Why would you," one of them added, "when it makes you feel so good?" The women of Wardie Bay have something of the warrior about them that epitomises the spirit of the wild swimmer: come rain, shine, hail or snow (often rain), they will be there in their numbers, supporting each other, laughing and dipping. What's not to love about this dedicated, consistent solidarity?

Our first swim on Barra was with Janette and her pals at their very own swim spot. They didn't tell us the name of their spot. These are smart women! But make no mistake, if you drive along the coast, you will find a spot to swim every fifteen seconds.

We went in off the rocks because the beach there can be too windy. Their spot was fantastic; the rocks were like steps into the sea and our introduction to island swimming was straight in at the deep end – and the deep end was cold. Way colder than we were used to. We were planning on swimming out to a nearby island, but very quickly Jeanette advised us against it given how choppy the sea was. These are the situations where you only listen, you never dispute. Jeanette knows the area incredibly well, and only a fool would disregard her advice. Thanks to the swim group, our introduction to island life was immediate. Jules observed that all the women have multiple jobs. This has traditionally been one of the distinctions that separates rural island life from city life. No one is just an actor, or only a nurse or nothing more than a teacher. An individual performs many functions on an island. Perhaps this is why swimming offers such a lovely, essential respite from the wearing of so many hats? Jeanette told us that whatever is going on, her group always makes time in their busy schedules to swim together twice a week.

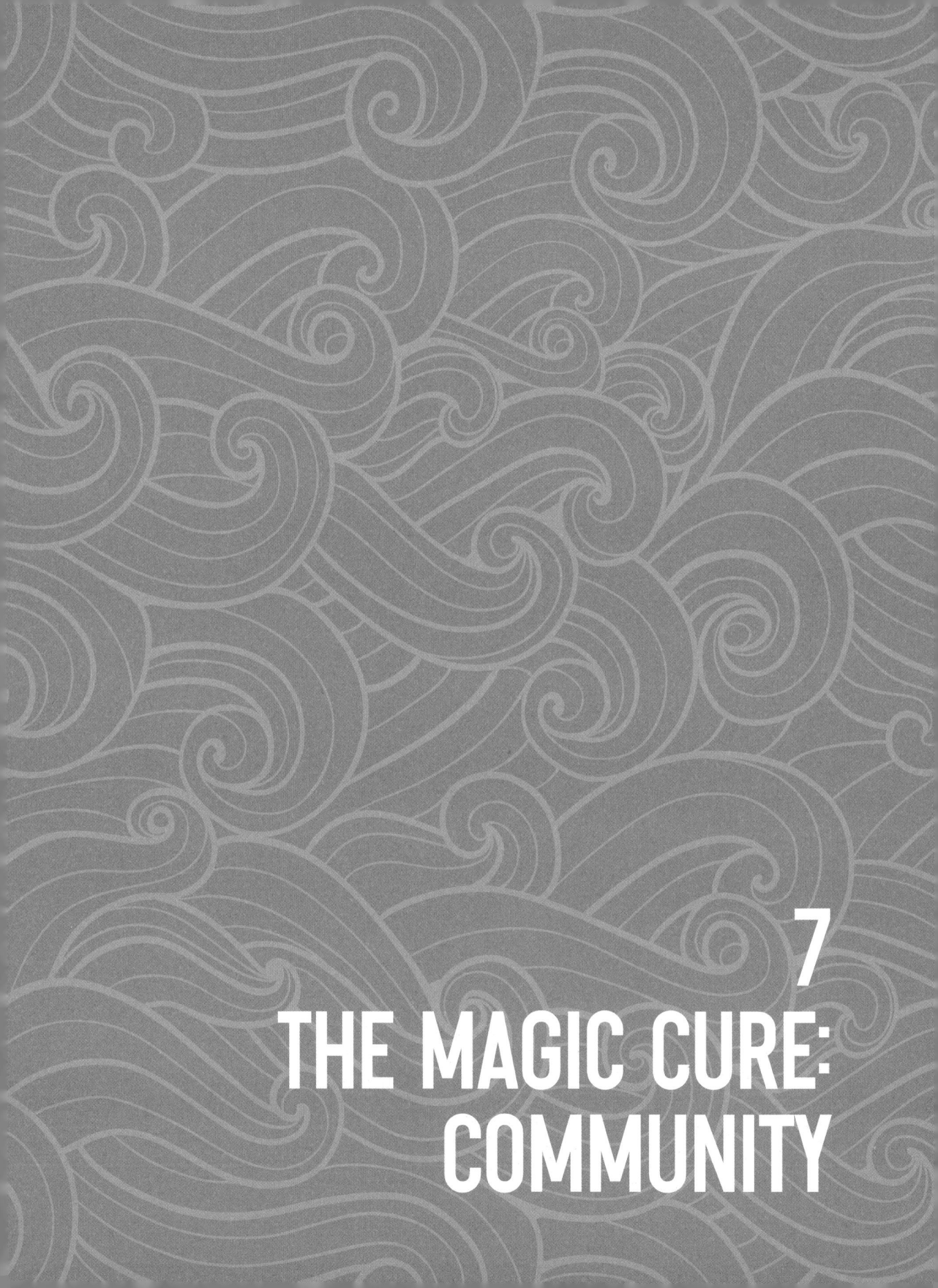

7
THE MAGIC CURE: COMMUNITY

YOUR SECOND CHILDHOOD

THE ISLAND FARMER WITH THE SAUNA

Our first swim took us via a farm where we met Hazel and Peter, a mother and son, who are farmers. Hazel told us about how stressful running a family farm is and how important dipping and swimming have been for her and how much this has helped with her mental health. Peter has recently started to join her in the water. Not only does she get to swim with her son and spend that time together, but he has also bought the best bit of kit any wild swimmer would love to have: a mobile sauna! In these exposed turquoise waters of Orkney, Hazel has now become the most popular member of her swim group! She is so proud of and knowledgeable about her island's rich history that we nearly frazzled ourselves in Peter's sauna listening to her stories of Orkney. When we eventually burst out the sauna looking like overcooked, steaming lobsters, the crew were trying to keep their equipment steady while they howled and shook with laughter.

small, red-roofed chapel transformed from two Nissen huts by Domenico Chiocchetti and his Italian POW colleagues. Sean Corbett, our cameraman, told us that his parents got married in this very chapel. Caught up in the romance of the moment, Jules asked director Tony if we had time in our schedule to nip in and renew our vows. Tony made a few phone calls and within hours we were stood in front of the local priest, John, who was happy to renew our vows with us. If there's one thing our wild swimming adventures have taught us both, it's to live in the moment. Having seen the Italian Chapel and heard its stories, we wondered when we would be back here again . . . and what exactly we were waiting for. So we decided between us to once again dive in. Magical Orkney had cast a spell on us, and the beautiful Italian Chapel was now part of our story too. We might not hurry back to Las Vegas, but we will definitely take our boys and our families to visit this incredible spot.

SWIMMING PLAYLIST

'THE SAME DEEP WATER AS YOU'
THE CURE

found ourselves in the gift shop buying pirate cups, T-shirts and, oh yes . . . rum. A beautiful, treacly Scottish rum that Greg insisted we had to try. Jules didn't need any warming up after the sauna, but tried it anyway and found it delicious. If you are ever on Orkney, pop in and visit the good people of J. Gow, and there you'll encounter island pirates with quite the formidable rum stash. PS. quite random, but they also make skateboards!

Do you remember our theory that life sometimes has a strange way of repeating itself – in a beautiful and satisfying way? So, for context, twenty-five years ago, 30 September 1999 to be precise, we eloped and got married in a hot-air balloon in Las Vegas. We enjoyed a couple of whiskies (not drunk but squiffy). Well, here we were, twenty-five years married (again, not drunk but squiffy) and standing outside a place called the Italian Chapel – a

to Sanday, we passed empty pillboxes guarding the surrounding seas as if they had been deserted a week ago. It's a very strange feeling of history from over eighty years ago being so palpable.

Done with swimming for the day, we discovered a rum distillery by the name of J. Gow (Of course Greg would find one on this trip!) named after a pirate and mutineer who commandeered a merchant ship called *Caroline* en route to Genoa and renamed her *The Revenge*. Greg likes reading about pirates and he really, *really* likes rum, so he made a strong argument for how important it was to support local start-up businesses and that's why we

LIFE REPEATS ITSELF

Orkney, a magical isle, really was an absolute change of pace from the get-go. I had never been, but Jules was returning here for the first time since 1994. She had finished a tour with TAG Theatre Company, which was a small touring company that travelled both its set and cast up and down the country in a red van, putting on shows in the community. Times like these are amazing cut-your-teeth days for a young actor as they serve as a real opportunity coming out of drama college to learn so much about theatre production. Jules still maintains that the touring experience gives you the groundwork and the knowledge to become a great theatre company member. You make friends for life, and you look after each other. (She can reel off the names of every actor she's ever toured with!)

Not unlike the swimming community, theatre is a family that sticks together, and, like that moment of stepping into the spotlight on opening night, that feeling of exposure, like taking off your dry robe on the beach for the first time, you get through a show together, you support each other and you realise you are all in great company; you are not on your own. Yes, there are a lot of similarities between a theatre group and a wild swimming group. There was a time, raising two kids and juggling a career, where Jules wondered if those carefree days of theatre touring adventure and silliness were behind her. It turns out that nothing could be further from the truth. Life has a funny habit of echoing itself and putting you in

touch with an earlier version of yourself, in a beautiful and satisfying way.

If you told Jules then that she would return here thirty years later with a Canadian husband and a BBC crew/family, making a show about wild swimming, throwing herself into the cold water and howling with laughter into her fifties, she wouldn't have believed you. Life takes many twists and turns. It truly is full of surprises, if you are open to it.

So, back to Orkney. The island is a history lovers' dream. The four Churchill Barriers and the stories of sunken Second World War vessels make it all seem so present, almost recent here. On the ferry

YOUR SECOND CHILDHOOD

> SWIM SPOT

STORNOWAY

Next was an amazing and memorable boat trip on an RIB (rigid inflatable boat) with Norma MacLeod and her husband Neil. We had swum with Immerse Hebrides before, but here we were meeting the big bosses. The top kiddies. The *capo di tutti i capi*. Norma and Neil do really cool swim excursions round the isles south of Stornoway. Norma revealed to us that she had recently had a cancer diagnosis. When she was going through chemotherapy the only thing she wanted to do was get down to the sea. Neil would take her there, and she would sit and just gaze out at it. This left her feeling cleansed. She feels now, having survived that, that she wants to fully embrace the sea and all its benefits, and make the most of the Immerse Hebrides venture. Such a lovely couple, we had a brilliant laugh with them, and they were a pleasure to spend time with. (Meanwhile, our crew once again hid expertly in the RIB. What must the people we talk to on this show think? Everywhere you look someone is curled up somewhere like a cat.) Norma was a brilliant and experienced guide, and her and Neil knew exactly what caves to take us to. We were followed all the way by a curious little seal that never came too close but also never left us.

As we jumped off the RIB with total strangers who were now friends, we talked about this incredible second childhood we were all having through swimming. It was quite a wild and remote experience, swimming amid huge ribbons of seaweed and beautiful aqua-green water that led us to the cave mouth. Norma encouraged us to put on our goggles and enjoy the view under the surface. A very cold swim but an unforgettable one.

Norma and Neil got us safely back to harbour and we said our goodbyes. This was the end of the Gaelic chapter of our adventure, but the wildness would continue . . .

sodden. Look, we don't pretend to be Bear Grylls here, but lying in a damp van after a long day shooting was not that fun. All we wanted was a dry sock. Each.

Jules made me smile through my miserable moaning by handing me a bugle. I didn't know she'd brought it. If you watch this episode, you might think, *Well, that was a bit random. Why does this guy have a bugle?* So here's the skinny. Jules and I recently watched the film *Nyad* (available to stream, starring Annette Bening and Jodie Foster), which tells the incredible tale of Diana Nyad, a swimmer with the ambition to cross the Florida Straits, a 110-mile body of water between Cuba and the Florida Keys. Nyad gives new meaning to the phrase "tough cookie" in her refusal to give up. She succeeded in her fifth attempt at the age of sixty-four. She also owned a bugle, which she used to blow at the beginning of her epic swims. I was totally taken with this and so Jules got her hands on a genuine Second World War bugle from Glasgow's Broadsword Antiques (whose famously outrageous next-door neighbour is Mr Ben Retro Clothing). The two stores are run by a couple called Robbie and Mary Ann, who happen to be two of our very good friends. I treasure this gift; Jules is an amazing and thoughtful gift giver. So there you have it. The story of the mysterious, not-so-random bugle.

TAKING ON NEW ADVENTURES TOGETHER

In Eriskay, we swam on the Coilleag a'Phrionnsa, on the west side of the island. There to meet us was the swim group Immerse Hebrides, a fabulous organisation which is run by Norma, who takes groups on wild swims in remote and unusual parts of the Hebrides. These guys are truly committed; they often swim three times a day. Safety is paramount for Norma and her group. They wear whistles, tow floats and do safety briefings before every swim. If you are looking to get in on the action, check out their website. People come from all over the world to swim with Norma's group. The day we met them we also met a lovely woman called Margot from Australia who told us, much to our surprise, that water temperatures in the Australian winter fall lower than water temperatures in the Scottish summer. Don't know why this seemed quite so surprising, but it did!

The next twenty-four hours were funny, and not always in a funny-ha-ha way. It was a brutal summer for poor weather, and this morning was a low point for both of us. You could see on our faces that we were struggling. The temperature had plunged; our van, Luke the Duke, had officially died after much protesting along the way; and it seemed that every single item of clothing we had brought with us was

incredible slice of island life. It was like we had left reality and stepped into the film *Local Hero*. We loved it.

I think the islanders felt they too had left reality. They were only in for a book of stamps and Jules was stood in the corner covering her boobs with two tea towels. Forget *Local Hero*, it was more like *Calendar Girls*. Thank God Benny and Chevy never saw any of this (they were still paddling away in the kayaks).

This was a bittersweet end to an episode as it was time to say goodbye (again) to Benny and Chevy, but the blow this time felt even harder because they were taking our dog Bonnie with them too. We would be carrying on our island adventure alone, just the two of us.

Again, the empty nest. Art imitating life.

tired of our patter, and running out of petrol had sent them over the edge.) Callum and Ellie work for their mum and dad's kayak business, Clearwater Paddling. They took us out to the only medieval castle in the Outer Hebrides, Kisimul Castle. We wanted to do something special with the boys before they left for Glasgow and they picked kayaking out to the castle. (Its name is derived from the Norse for "castle island", which gives you a clue as to our transport choice.) Paddling out to the castle marked the one and only time Chevy joined us in the water on the show, and it was very memorable. If you ever visit Barra, you really should look up Callum and Ellie and do this magical excursion. (You can take a ferry to Oban from this very bay.)

After a brief history lesson courtesy of Callum and Ellie, we swam back. The water was particularly open for a bay, making it choppy and brown and peaty.

This swim was one of the few times on our show when, to be honest, we were making it up as we went along. Arriving back on shore, we didn't have any of the precious kit we keep banging on about, not a towel between us, but in true island style we were saved by Janette (our pal from our very first swim), who runs the post office/café. Janette brought us inside straight off the jetty, dried us off with tea towels, and gave us a huge pot of tea and a plate of chittery bites so vast that it would choke a horse. We stood there dripping wet in the middle of the post office. An

At this point, we'd just like to give a special shout-out to our director Tony Kearney and producer Jim Webster. Firstly, for having the foresight to keep a spare canister of petrol in the back of the van but, secondly, for their next-level talents. You might not realise it, but it took four days to film the episode on Barra. Tony's skill is taking hours and hours of footage and building a story thread to tie in all the best bits and present them in a mere twenty-eight minutes. He made it look like all those swims happened in the one day. They didn't. We are too old for that. We would be knackered.

So, kidding on this was the same day, off the four of us went to meet Callum and Ellie. (Our sons met us there. They were

water, the warmer the air seems when you come out. When you emerge from freezing waters onto a beach, you feel like you are in the Bahamas for a few minutes, which is always an enjoyable experience, but make no mistake, this is an illusion, created by your blood ferociously firing round your core. Don't be lulled into a false sense of security in these moments. Get dry, get that loose kit on (easy-to-pull-on clothes – warm joggies, baggy sweat shorts, big socks or easy-to-pull-on boots. No skinny jeans, etc.!) and get properly warm. (And don't forget the best bit, the chittery bite!)

We said goodbye to Ishi, but before we did, she recommended a bakery honesty box called Piece of Cake. You read that right. You rock up to the bakery box, open it and help yourself to a variety of amazing cakes. You are trusted to be honest enough to leave the cake cash in a tin. Lo and behold, Chevy, who hadn't swum with us yet, was all about this cake box. We spent about twenty-five quid on baked goods for him alone.

the dangerous nature of their journey. This monument felt like a reminder to us both of our responsibility with this TV programme of ours, to take great care when entering bodies of water, especially the sea. The safety element is so important, especially when we are encouraging people of so many levels of swimming ability to enter the water. Straight off the bat, this second series always felt different from the first: the swims felt that bit harder, especially the Atlantic-side swims as compared to the swims on the island's leeward side. Safety was even closer to the forefront of our minds than in previous episodes, and this monument was a stark reminder of the sea's power.

We never needed our kit more than the swim we went on with Ishi. This was one of those lovely occasions where we were all soaked before we had even started. We met Ishi on a bench at a café next to where we were swimming and within five minutes the Scottish weather had soaked us through. Ishi is a delight. An islander born and bred, she had come full circle after having travelled the world and returned home. The circle was most evident given that she was now teaching Gaelic in the very classroom where she'd first learned it. The only difference for Ishi was as a little girl she'd learned to swim in the swimming pool that was built in Barra in the early 1990s, but now she's shed the pool habit and prefers to do her swimming in the sea.

Our swim with Ishi was extreme. We had an offshore wind lashing us into the beautiful crystal-clear green water, and us city softies had to put on a brave face in front of Ishi, but this was much tougher than anything we were used to. Ishi was very eloquent and spoke poetically about why she swims. She said, "The world looks better from in here." Benny came in with us on this swim and said it was the coldest swim he'd ever had in his life (Chevy knew better than to even put a toe in.). But he still stayed in there with us and spoke about how amazing he felt on exiting the water. The strange thing about these swims is that the colder the

SWIMMING PLAYLIST

'LIKE SWIMMING'
FOALS

ISLAND HOPPING WITH OUR BOYS

Special shout-out to the multiple causeways throughout the Hebrides. Our director Tony was telling us that the plan was, eventually, to have all the islands linked, which would be amazing for communities and local businesses alike, not to mention tourists. Imagine a kind of chilly, but chiller, Florida Keys! Very cool indeed. We travelled over our first Hebridean causeway to Vatersay to meet Ishi. Before that, we stopped off at the Annie Jane monument. This beautiful stone monument stands above Vatersay west beach – Traigh Shiar in Gaelic. The *Annie Jane* was en route from Liverpool (where Jules's family is from) and headed to Quebec (where Greg's family is from) when it demasted on the Atlantic side of Vatersay. Three hundred and fifty people, heading to the new world, lost their lives. We were moved by this monument. It felt strange to us that we both had a familial connection to the two points on this ship's route, and, looking over the bay, we got a sense of the vastness of the ocean that lay in front of those who perished and

GREG

My two cents on the matter of the empty nest is very similar to Jules's, but what's most painful for me is watching her go through it. I remember growing up in Canada, where loads of my friends' parents seemed to get divorced once their kids went to college. I've thought about that often, as it seems all too easy to fall into the trap of feeling as though your only purpose in life is to serve the kids. Once that "job" is complete, your partner can feel like a stranger. My biggest fear was that our kids would bugger off, Jules would turn to me and go: "Christ. Is this what I've got to look forward to? Thirty more years with YOU?" To be fair, that could still happen. I can be very annoying.

But since the boys left home and the nest became empty but for us two, I feel like we have both been far more attentive, in a good way, towards the other. (Maybe Jules thinks "*Christ!*" about this too?) Checking in on each other, making cups of tea without being asked, going on weekends away together and taking up a hobby together. (Which is why we are sitting here right now, writing this book. Correction: I am writing; she is on her phone.) We plan to take up golf next. Neither of us have ever lifted a golf club in our lives. What a laugh it will be. A guaranteed giggle. Learning how to drive together, play the fairway together, get out the bunker together, and putt together. I have a feeling she's going to be very good at it.

Anyways, we are not a couple of lonely old sad sacks JUST yet. About an hour ago, we found out that both our boys are descending on us this Friday night. We will be cooking up a massive pot of spaghetti Bolognese, and I made them agree to a game of Monopoly in the Hemphill WhatsApp group. It will be a fun family night, with the gang all together, as if they never left. And I will crush them all.

YOUR SECOND CHILDHOOD

And those feelings have bonded me even more tightly to my swimming community because if I swim tomorrow with someone I don't know and they happen to mention that their kid's left home and gone off to university, then I genuinely know pretty much what they're going through and am able to offer comfort and support, just like Lorraine did for me that day. Cold water swimming on these occasions is community and therapy and unexpected human connections all in one.

Enjoy them ordering late-night pizza after you've made them dinner which they've barely touched, enjoy them swearing like the proverbial troopers on their Xbox headsets at two in the morning. Enjoy them staying in the shower for forty minutes then leaving the bathroom like it was hit by a particularly steamy tsunami. Enjoy them never taking the garbage out. Enjoy their jogger-clad arses sticking out of your fridge as they hunt for random snacks. Enjoy them driving you crazy. Enjoy them delighting you with their teenage nonsense because all of their infuriating, endearing habits are a million times better than the silence of them not being there.

stupidly went for lunch which neither of us could eat. (I am actually crying remembering this, for Christ's sake.) Then it came time to leave, and the sight of him at his wee student window, waving me off, nearly did me in. On the way back to Glasgow, I was in bits, but I was saved by my beautiful pal, Lorraine, who had already been through this three times previously. (And mercifully, she did not warn me about how difficult and shite it was going to be.) She was amazing. I was inconsolable, but she just talked. She made me laugh, she made me breathe, she let me ball my eyes out, and she supported me and got me back to Glasgow safely. She was my navigator, my emotional autopilot. That's what friends are for. I'm lucky to have great ones.

The empty nest doesn't just happen to you for a day; it is a shift in your role as a parent, a milestone that is inevitable from the very beginning. The difficulty, I think, for any parent is accepting that once they are gone, they are gone. Even when they come back, which so many do, it's different. I wasn't an empty nester only on that day, I still am and I am still adjusting every day. For me, my cold water swimming is an invaluable crutch. A dose of medicine on days when I'm really missing the kids.

WHEN THE NEST IS EMPTY

JULES

That night we hit the campsite at Wavecrest and enjoyed some ridiculously tasty fish and chips from the Fishbox Kitchen van. It was bittersweet filming with our boys because they had both moved out the previous September within a space of about two weeks. It would be an understatement to say that our heads were still spinning from their respective departures. We talked in the show about this strange period of transition that nearly all parents go through. It seems there are times in a woman's life that women feel honour bound to protect other women from, by ensuring they know what needs to be known in any way possible. Pregnancy, miscarriage, relationship failure, childbirth, breastfeeding, guilt over working as a parent, guilt in general, dealing with an elderly parent, dealing with your partner's grief and, of course, the syndrome of the empty nest. It's just there doesn't seem to be quite so much chat about how that empty nest feels.

Now even though I went through this process of the boys leaving home with Greg, it was far worse for me. FACT. I stand by this statement because I grew them in my body for nine months, then they came out my vagina. (Well, one of them did anyway.) Then they fed off my breasts for six months a piece. Not that it's a competition, but I win. Sit down, Greg.

Dropping Chevy at uni was an awful day. Greg was filming, so I was on my own. I moved him in, put all his stuff out, then we

EMBRACING MIDDLE AGE

JULES

Coming to Tobermory, I was struck by a profound thought. There is a constant to the sea. It bears no grudge towards you if you ignore it. Which I did. I never once dipped so much as a toe in the water here in my twenties. But the sea waited for me until I was ready. It wasn't until I was in my fifties, menopausal, dealing with elderly parents, dealing with kids, that I entered the waters round Tobermory Bay for the first time. There I am, swimming by the multicoloured houses, at one with the sea and . . . oh wait. Maybe it does bear a grudge. How do you fancy a bunch of sore jellyfish stings up your legs? And why exactly has it taken you twenty years to get in this water, you couple of absolute cowardly fannies?

We finished off filming our final chat by the fire, surrounded by the crew, but we had a little surprise for Tony and the crew who had set up the camera behind us. We asked him if he would keep running. We had been talking for three weeks about caring less, embracing middle age and shedding our inhibitions. We had watched an Italian film, a few weeks before, about a couple. The guy is trying to bring the girl out of herself and back to feeling young again. She has lost her sense of being a free spirit. Out of nowhere, the girl stands, strips and runs into the sea and he follows suit. We thought it would be funny to recreate the scene from the film. This seemed like a good idea given that the camera was behind us, but we hadn't thought about coming back out the water. You were mercifully spared that footage.

YOUR SECOND CHILDHOOD

IONA

Jules had arranged to swim with Fiona and her pals while we visited Iona. Fiona's grandparents were from Iona, and they were great believers in the sea curing all ills. Her grandma swam on this very beach into her nineties. If that's not a recommendation, we don't know what is. Finishing series one on such a beautiful and magical island felt unforgettable for us.

for four years, nobody suggested we did, or seemed to be doing, wild swimming. I spent loads of time on the water on excursions on sightseeing boats, RNLI boats, trips to Fingal's Cave, and despite having spent a lot of time at Calgary Bay, I was never inclined to go for a swim. Twenty years later, that reluctance seems unimaginable to me.

It's funny that, at fifty-one, I feel braver and fitter and more willing to enter freezing waters than in my twenties. Most sport, when you think about it, you tend to start in your youth, and then as you grow older, you ease back on it or even give it up. Perhaps, I wondered, wild swimming is the reverse of that? There is something *Cocoon*-like about what we do. (Young ones, if you don't know what we're talking about, go and rent this from your local Blockbusters.) There is something in the water that rejuvenates you.

THE BOOKSHELF

THE TIDAL YEAR
BY FREYA BROMLEY

JULES & GREG'S WILD SWIM

later. Me and the entire *Balamory* cast are still in touch. We started a WhatsApp group a few months back because, lo and behold, two decades since the show was first aired, *Balamory* is to return to our screens in 2026. The best thing about the revival so far is this WhatsApp group.

We were barely off the ferry and with just one look out the window at the array of beautiful, coloured houses, I was in tears. Every shop seemed to have *Balamory*-related merch in the window, so wild swimming was going to have to take a back seat while I enjoyed my homecoming moment of glory.

Somehow I couldn't get my head round the fact that, having effectively lived there

JULES

During filming, we had the opportunity to return to Mull. Mull is very special for both of us. Twenty or so years previously, I had spent my summers here filming the children's TV show *Balamory*. I'd not long had a baby, our first son Benny, who is now twenty-three and a giant at six foot five. He was just seven months old when we brought him up to Mull so that I could work but not be separated from him for long periods. When Greg wasn't able to stay, I had Mum and Dad on hand to look after the wee one. We felt so lucky to be working and have family there to help look after our little lad.

Mull in the summer is a truly incredible place. It doesn't get dark until about 11.30 p.m., and we had four summers there making memories that we would treasure forever. This was a special time in our lives. *Balamory* and *Still Game* started shooting the same month! Little did we know then that we would be working on shows that would change our lives and that people would still be talking about twenty-five years later.

One of the aspects of our jobs that we really love is the bonds we make. With our fellow actors, the crew and the locals, who often become friends for life. Andy Agnew, who plays PC Plum, would become godfather to our second son, Chevy, four years

childhood" in a very real and profound way. It reminds me every day just how much I loved the water as a kid. Others were comfortable standing on a baseball diamond or a soccer pitch; in the deep end at Fairview pool was where I was most at home. It was my happy place.

I spoke to Sally about it that day, and I think for so many people, swimming once more connects them to their childhood. It takes them back to a time of playfulness and the wonderful, carefree abandon that we all eventually give up as we enter adulthood and ease ourselves into a life of responsibility.

Two seconds from the glorious swimming spot that Sally had taken us to, you will find Taymouth Marina, our home for the next two nights. Jules had booked us into the spa for an end-of-shoot treat. The Taymouth Marina worked its magic and we were sorry to leave. In fact, Jules was so relaxed the next day, she nearly crashed the car manoeuvring out of a parking spot. Watching the show back, we are reminded that the cameras are rolling the entire time. That means there are times when you are aware you are on camera and times when you forget. And at one point what you see is a genuine married-couple squabble, which our director Tony found hilarious and decided to put into the show. Jules and I trust Tony, and we saw the funny side. The last thing we want for anybody who decides to watch the show is to come away from it thinking that we are some perfect couple. (She drives me crazy and I annoy the hell out of her on a daily basis. But we do laugh a lot together, and that is like couples' medicine.)

YOUR SECOND CHILDHOOD

GREG

Sally spoke beautifully about how she has swum through her grief at losing her mother. Like Lee, she often takes herself off on her own to be alone with her thoughts.

Swimming for me is also firmly connected to my parents. Growing up in Canada, I swam every day in the summer during the small window when the water is warm enough. I remember wonderful long summer days at Fairview municipal pool, a great centre of the community and a wonderful hub to keep young active minds occupied and out of trouble.

I often joke with Jules about how I "almost" swam for Canada. The truth is a little less exciting. My school pal Jeff and I were offered bursaries to train all year round and Jeff took up the challenge, whereas I did not. It would involve two two-hour swimming sessions a day, one before school and one after. It was a real fork-in-the-road moment for me, as I knew deep down I just didn't have that kind of physical commitment or belief in me. I remember seeing Jeff through the winter, pink eyed and falling asleep at his desk. While I admired him, I knew I had made the right choice for me.

Swimming for this TV show is a weird full-circle moment for me. It has connected me to what I like to call my "second

BEHIND THE SCENES

The scenery had to be put on hold as we had a major outbreak of midgie malice. One of the perils of filming on the West Coast of Scotland in the summer is you can get eaten alive at dawn and dusk. I don't know what it is about these times that sets the wee buggers off, but it is nigh on impossible to function during these short windows. Jules recalls shooting *Balamory* in Mull, and just before a take the entire cast would remove their head nets on the shout of "Action!" They would rattle through their lines as quickly as they could, then as soon as the cry of "Cut!" went up, the crew would run in and re-hood the actors before they got eaten alive. Torture. The glamour of TV.

YOUR SECOND CHILDHOOD

Neither of us really fancied having a midlife crisis. Instead, wild swimming has given us a wonderful opportunity in midlife – a second childhood, if you will.

During the filming of series one of the show, we joined Sally Reid for a swim at Kenmore, a place steeped in her family history. Sally is our pal through acting. Both Jules and I have worked with her over the years, and it's her who we started the secret splinter swim group with when we were all in Glasgow together. We have a riot when we gather for a swim, and the emphasis is on laughter and patter, of which there is plenty.

A swim with Sally always puts a smile on your face, but today was more heartfelt as she explained that we were swimming in a spot that was close to her heart. She had swum here as a kid with her brother, her mum and dad, and her granny. The bridge at Kenmore looks like something out of a film. You are right at the meeting point between the River Tay and Loch Tay.

6
YOUR SECOND CHILDHOOD

dip so enjoyable. We marvelled at how eloquently she spoke about her son Joe, especially when she said she was sure he wanted her to think about him but for her, above all, to be happy. You can't just wake up and be happy; you have to work at it – and Lee was. For her, cold water swimming was not some fun escapade taking place at a surface level, but something deeper and genuinely essential to her wellbeing. Out of everyone we have swum with in the last few years, Lee's story stands out for so many people. She is a shining example of the myriad reasons as to why people take to the water. Cold water swimming is about coming out of your comfort zone and, that day, Lee did it with courage and grace. We felt so privileged that Lee felt comfortable enough with us to share her heartfelt story. Jules knew she had connected with a new pal that day. Jules and Lee have dipped together several times at Mugdock since and still keep in touch.

JULES & GREG'S WILD SWIM

THE BOOKSHELF

WINTERING
BY KATHERINE MAY

ON THE TIDES OF GRIEF AND LOSS

DEALING WITH FAMILY ILLNESS

We swam with a wonderful woman called Lee. Jules had come across Lee's story in the newspaper and passed her details on to our director. Lee's reason for swimming was to try and heal herself in the water from the tragic loss of her son Joe, who was eleven years old when he passed away from a rare cancer. Lee's support network took her for a group swim. When she was in the water she started to cry, and when she came out she noticed that something had shifted. After this, she found it easier to swim alone, finding that when she is in the water, she feels close to Joe. Her beloved swim spot turned out to be Abie's Loch in Mugdock Park. She also found that taking her camera and logging her swims felt extremely beneficial to her wellbeing, and she often augmented her swims by taking photos underwater. When we swam with her, she was taking our picture too. We were both unsure if she wanted to come on camera and tell her story, because she had developed into a solo swimmer, but in the end we had no need to worry. As a solo dipper, Lee always tells a loved one where and when she's dipping. This is obviously really important for an individual swimmer's safety.

The White Loch is a very peaty and deep swim. Some serious swimmers can be found doing laps of the loch. As a dip, it can be quite challenging due to the lack of shelter and the elevated level of the site, but it's a beautiful swim with an open aspect mere minutes from the city. Even though it was cold, Lee made the

SWIM SPOT

A SWIM AND A SLICE OF PIZZA

In Orkney, our friend Adam took us to what can only be described as an empty beach. It looked as if it had been years since another soul had even walked along it. It might have been properly deserted, but as soon as we entered the water, we immediately discovered we were being watched. Adam told us that the local seals always appeared when anyone entered the water. They were curious but cautious as they kept their distance while watching us with their big dark eyes. Jules spent the entire time trying to commune with them; honestly, she could make friends anywhere, this woman! As if this day couldn't have got any better, afterwards Adam took us to a pizza shack. (That's right, you read that correctly.) Billed as the most northerly pizza joint in the British Isles, 59 Degrees North is well worth your time if you find yourself on Orkney. We received such a warm welcome at this little restaurant built around a huge, impressive stone pizza oven, as we sat and talked with Sanday's community of wild swimmers. Such a lovely bunch, we have promised to return there and swim with them in some of their favourite spots. It was a memorable end to a wonderful day, eating what can only be described as the greatest chittery bite we've had so far!

SWIMMING PLAYLIST

'SWIMMING'
BREATHE OWL BREATHE

JULES & GREG'S WILD SWIM

of fifty-four. Euan told us that swimming really has helped him through some hard times, and now he needs to swim every day.

One of the things about Euan is that he is a solo swimmer. Jules and I always admire the solo swimmers. They don't have the group to encourage them; they only have their own discipline to heed the alarm clock, get out of bed and muster the willpower to grab the trunks (or cossie) and towel and get down there. Euan says his swim sets him up for his day ahead, and he has become a local fixture for the community on those cold mornings. Folk like to keep an eye out for him on his morning swims!

ON THE TIDES OF GRIEF AND LOSS

We have met many people over the last couple of years who have spoken to us so beautifully about how they swim in order to cope with their grief. We've heard stories about how when they enter the water, it's like a tap being turned on and they feel able to release something. We've heard it said that once in the water they feel closer to the person they have lost, especially when they used to spend time in or on the water with them.

SWIMMING THROUGH GRIEF

Our last day of filming on series two of *Jules & Greg's Wild Swim* was in Shetland – the furthest-away place we'd ever swum before. We started off in the historic part of Lerwick town at South End Beach, accompanied by Euan the postie. We were joining him for his "alarm clock" swim: his alarm clock being the morning ferry. Euan explained his reasons for swimming. He began raising money for charity when his dad succumbed to Alzheimer's at the age

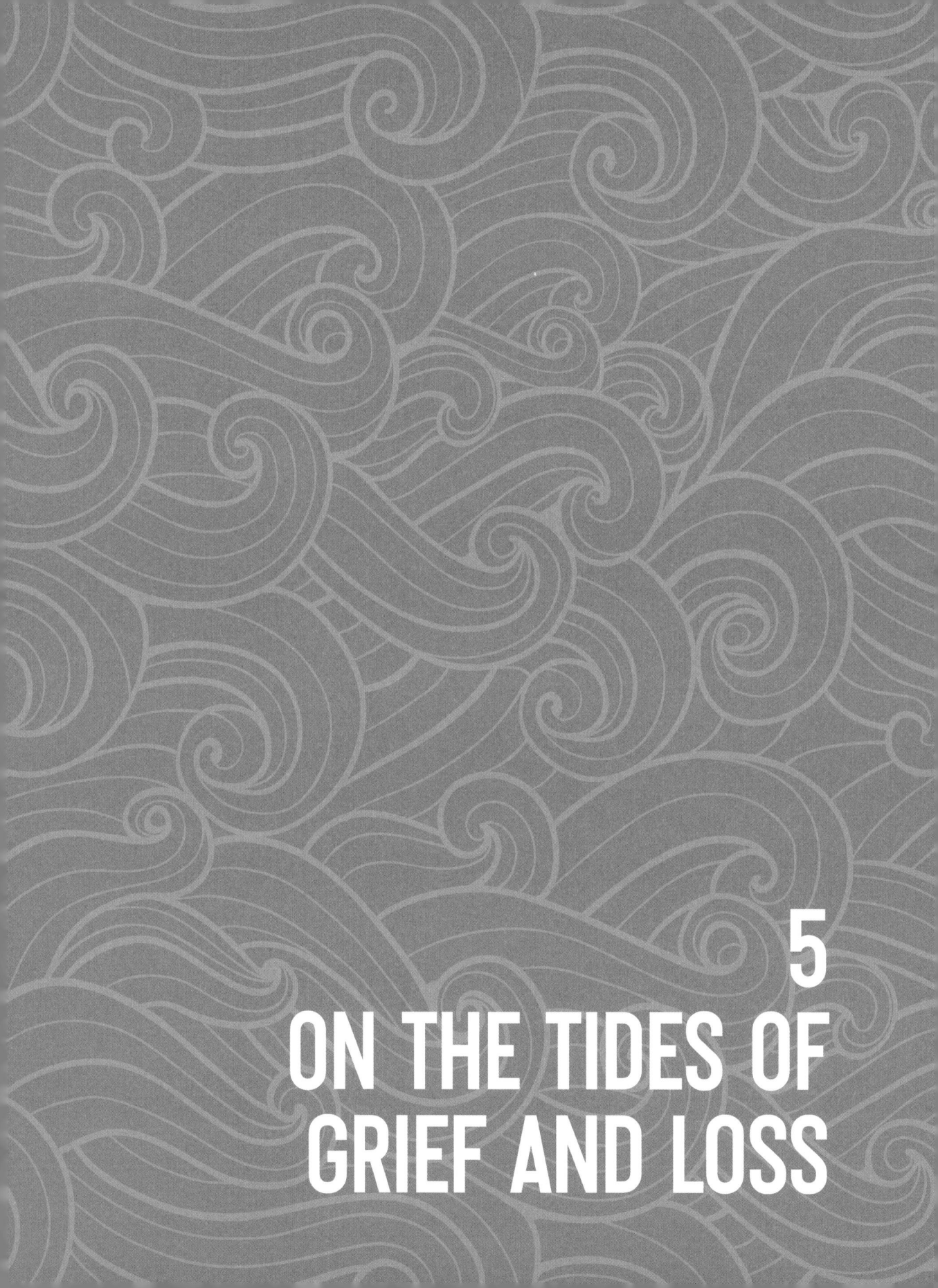

5
ON THE TIDES OF GRIEF AND LOSS

SOUL SOOTHING

SWIM SPOT

ARDNAMURCHAN PENINSULA

Special shout-out to a special place. If you look closely at one of Jules's (admittedly numerous) hats, you'll see a lighthouse knitted into the fabric. This particular hat was bought on the Ardnamurchan Peninsula, which is the most remote and westerly peninsula of the British mainland. If you get a chance, go and explore this part of Scotland. It is a little (well, a lot) off the beaten track and all the better for it. A beautiful single-track drive and incredible scenery round every bend AND you end up at Corrachadh Mòr, the most westerly point and home to the Ardnamurchan Lighthouse, as featured on Jules's hat. Go and check out this incredible part of Scotland, the geology of which was formed from a volcano erupting some sixty million years ago. It has white-sand bays, a nature reserve, ancient settlements and a distillery, and its craggy beauty is truly breathtaking.

JULES & GREG'S WILD SWIM

SOUL SOOTHING

SLOW DOWN AND TAKE A BREATH

During filming, we found ourselves in Glen Brittle, on the Isle of Skye, to have a swim with Josh, a traveller who had found work at the campsite there. Josh is a hardy young fellow whose company we enjoyed. The waterfall he took us to was one of the coldest swims we'd had so far. You have to remember, this is fast-flowing water coming straight off the mountain. As well as Greg falling on his arse on the way down, Jules took her eye off the ball and got swept down a natural rockslide, which had been worn away by the water for an age. She tumbled down to the next water pool. Fortunately for her, the cameras were not rolling. We both felt like big kids on this swim. Jumping in, diving under and getting tumbled about in an ice-cold washing machine. A most refreshing swim! And Josh himself was brilliantly refreshing company; unusually for a teenager, he's turned his back on social media. He talked about living in the moment and how he didn't want to miss what was right in front of him. Josh had an old head on young shoulders.

After this experience, we realised that wild swimming is great because it forces you to be in the moment. Just breathing, feeling that cold water on your skin, moving one stroke after another. Put your phone away and just be here. It feels incredible.

SOUL SOOTHING

SWIM TIP

"THE CHITTERY BITE"

What on earth, you ask, is a *chittery bite*? Well, it has many names; some call it a shivery bite, others call it a sweet treat or a reward or even the "best bit" of the dip. To boil it down for you, it's anything sweet that's homemade or shop bought that can be easily consumed (or "hoovered" or "inhaled") to take the edge off that cold feeling that can descend after a swim. In most swimming groups, there are always a couple of dippers whose chittery bite game is impressively strong. Look out for people with proper Tupperware boxes. They are next-level contenders. Chittery bite rituals are always a good laugh and can often resemble an aquatic version of the *Great British Bake Off*.

JULES & GREG'S WILD SWIM

Hannah and Callum are passionate about wellbeing, mental health and making a real difference in the traditional Shetland community. They're using their saunas to reach out to many different communities including LGBTQ+, guys only, menopausal women and other groups. Their method is sauna first, then into the cold ocean, then back into the heat, then into the other side of the tombolo, then back into the heat to finish. The two bodies of water on either side of the tombolo couldn't be more different. We noticed straight away that one was as still and steady as glass (North Sea), while the other was choppy and wild (Atlantic Ocean) The choppy side looked colder, but it wasn't, as it had the advantage of being warmed by the Gulf Stream. The glassy calm water, which you might have thought would be warmer, was actually bloody freezing! Hannah and Callum's aim with these saunas is to "rejuvenate", and we can testify to feeling that way after an afternoon spent in this beautiful setting. Jules and I couldn't think of a better place to finish the series.

the swimming community, but beyond that, with the wider local community. It seemed like everyone we met knew her. She gifted us two hats, knitted by her and her mum, telling us we couldn't swim on Shetland without a Shetland wool cap. Jules was so moved and happy to add yet another woolly bonnet to her burgeoning collection!

Emma was full of surprises. She took us to a longhouse where we sat and shared a chittery bite by the fire with a group of local Vikings. There we learned about Shetland's Viking heritage and Up Helly Aa, the annual fire festival that takes place at the end of January to mark the passing of another winter. We have promised to attend one year, though we are not entirely sure our livers will be able to keep pace.

Our final swim of *Jules & Greg's Wild Swim* series two was in the south-west of Lerwick, Shetland, at a famous spot named St Ninian's Isle. This is a natural sand causeway known as a tombolo beach, which connects two land masses with water on both sides. It's so beautiful it's almost hard to look at. We were excited to meet a lovely couple there, named Hannah and Callum, who are known in the swimming world as the original sauna bosses. Since they have returned from living in Norway for years, a project during Covid sprang to life: to bring sauna culture to the west side of Shetland.

SWIMMING PLAYLIST

**'FRONT CRAWL'
FRANK TURNER**

we had never seen before. Comfort, fashion, fleece-lined; we guarantee that your legs will never feel warmer. It's even got a safety whistle for if you get into bother. What's not to like here? For the record, we do not receive or solicit endorsements or free stuff, but you can bet your bottom dollar that two of these knockout suits were purchased from an amazing chandlery in Lerwick. We gifted them to each other as anniversary presents. Romantic, eh?

Emma's swim spot is one of the most breathtaking, memorable and eye-catching locations we have ever witnessed. The crew couldn't wait to start filming. We were the only humans for miles around, and all we had for company were thousands of birds which dived down into the water as we swam around, presumably because we were disturbing the fish. It felt like something out of *Jurassic Park*. We wish we'd known then about the fabulous Merlin app; if you are curious about bird life, is a fantastic asset that can spot birds for you by photo or sound. We are addicted to it.

Emma pointed out something very cool and unexpected. The surrounding rocks were ancient but soft. Over the years they had dispersed and been absorbed into the beach. If you rub this sand on yourself, you basically look like Edward from *Twilight* (or Ziggy Stardust if you are too old for that reference).

Emma told us how she'd learned to swim in the sea when she was three years old, when she was a "pirrie lass" ("pirrie" being the Shetland word for wee – or small). She taught all her brothers and sisters to swim. Now she swims for herself, to help her cope with her menopause and the stresses of her busy work life as a nurse. She is heavily involved in

THE BOOKSHELF

THE LITTLE BOOK FOR WILD SWIMMERS BY LAURA SILVERMAN

THE FEEL-GOOD FACTOR

We've been all over Scotland for *Jules & Greg's Wild Swim* – an adventure that has taken us as far north as Shetland.

Our first swim there was the most extreme we've ever done. We had to travel quite a distance to get to Unst. (Two ferries. Bloody worth it though.) We were very excited to meet a local legend by the name of Emma Williamson, who is an A&E nurse and an onset unit nurse of the BBC drama *Shetland*, which was shot here for nearly ten years. Emma has taken great pals of ours swimming up here, over the years. Before we even came to Shetland, we were told we needed to hook up with her. Jules befriended her on Instagram (what would we do without social media?), and the rest is history.

Emma took us to her favourite swim spot, Burra Firth, which also happens to be the most northerly swim we have done so far for the show. Turns out Emma is fit as a fiddle, and she marched us for what seemed like miles to her swim spot. Jules saw this as an opportunity to find out more about Emma's fantastic all-weather gear. That is, the legendary Fladen flotation suit. Basically, a boiler suit, the likes of which

By now, you've hopefully got the gist – wild swimming is incredibly good for you. It keeps you fit and healthier for longer, for sure, but what we really want to emphasise is how good it can make you feel, not just in your body but in your mind.

On our journey through wild swimming, we've met some wonderful people from all walks of life, and many have had their own mental health difficulties, from depression to addiction and everything in between. As we've seen in Chapter 3, mental health is not always easy to talk about – particularly for men – which is one of the reasons that we are so passionate about this topic.

For Jules, cold water dipping has been invaluable to her mental health. There has been so much coverage about the physical symptoms of the menopause and perimenopause – and she talks a lot in the programme about hot flushes and how much the cold water has helped her with them – but there is less said about the brain fog and mental health impact of the menopause, which can be incredibly debilitating. Let's face it, anything you can do, when you are suffering with your mental health, that takes you into the realm of physical and outdoors into nature, is going to give you a boost. This is surely far and away one of the top reasons why people keep coming back to wild swimming time and again.

4
SOUL SOOTHING

MEN SUPPORTING MEN

Over the last couple of years, one of our sons, Benny, has joined us on our swims more and more – and it was always lovely to have him along. He speaks openly about the benefits that swimming has on his own mental health, and on a few occasions, he's even managed to talk his pals into having a dip in the cold tub in our back garden. We get through a lot of towels on those days! Anyone who cold water dips cannot help but have noticed the increase in groups of young men taking part. Jules speaks in the show about how heartening she finds this, particularly as the mother of two sons.

JULES & GREG'S WILD SWIM

STAR SWIMMERS
DUNDEE DOOKERS

While filming the rivers episode of *Jules & Greg's Wild Swim*, we had our first dip in the White Loch at Broughty Ferry. We were greeted by Stephen and his group, the Dundee Dookers, an LGBTQ+ group of men from the local area. Men supporting men is the mantra of this fun and friendly bunch. They are well organised and have upped their game with some brilliant merch – we both got T-shirts – and a very welcoming Facebook page for those who may be "cold swim curious". They meet just along from the castle at Broughty Ferry, in front of the RNLI lifeguard station. This group really highlights how encouraging and accepting the wild-swimming community is. Give them a shout if you're thinking of taking the plunge!

hand on heart, I would actively encourage any guy out there who's struggling with their own mental health to connect with such groups.

My entry into wild swimming was, I confess, typically male. I took an age to move through all the phases. You might recognise these:

1) That's not for me.
2) Youse are all off your nuts.
3) There's definitely a glow about you. Maybe I'll come along one day.
4) Maybe I'll come and hold your jacket and watch.
5) Right I'll try it, stop going on about it.
6) Hold MY jacket.
7) This is bloody freezing.
8) This is bloody magic!

In my five years as a born-again swimmer, I can honestly say I am a different person. I feel so much better within myself. I have shed any body consciousness that hit me in my mid-fifties (I am far more focused on feeling better than worrying about how I look). I have made a hat load of new pals, and I feel this (frankly weird) sense of peace within myself.

I credit that initial, and subsequent, immersion in cold water with forcing me to open up. To open up with Jules and my boys. I want to be a better communicator with them, and I think the water has made me better at expressing myself. (I do wonder, though, if this might be because when you are standing there freezing, it seems like talking and yammering might just warm you up!)

> **STAR SWIMMERS**
> ## SOUL SUITES
>
> In Jules's hometown of East Kilbride, a group of young men have started a group named Soul Suites. These young pals wanted to create a space of "health and wellbeing" in response to losing so many friends to suicide. They are setting up hiking trips, football games, meditation, infrared saunas and cold water plunges all in the simple pursuit of feeling better. Their mission is so vital and necessary. Check them out on socials: @soulsuites. They now have branches in both East Kilbride and Hamilton.

GUY TALK

Being involved in this programme (and being a father of two young men) has given me a real insight into the modern attitudes to mental health held by the next generation of men. It seems to me that although they might not gather together in the same ways that we did in our youth (mainly in the pub or maybe on the football pitch), they are far better equipped at going deeper with one another and talking frankly about depression, anxiety and their mental health in ways that we never did. But I'm sure the good folk of the many male swimming groups that exist in Scotland and beyond would agree, with male suicide on the rise (in 2023, in Scotland, males remain three times as likely to die by suicide than females), we are only scratching the surface of the problem. There is much more work to be done. The men I've met in groups like the Dundee Dookers and the Edinburgh Blue Balls are shining examples of a new wave of men capable of gathering and sharing the weight of whatever burdens they find themselves suffering under. In that respect, the many groups of male swimmers are nothing short of inspirational. And

Later that night we reflected on the day. Jules and I were both quiet and in a contemplative mood. We decided to take Bonnie for a walk and have a drink at the pub, where it all came out. What if we're the wrong people to be listening to these stories? What do we know about this generation's battles, whether it's anxiety or troubling mental health? We don't have degrees in this stuff; we're actors, for Christ's sake. What if we say the wrong thing? We both talked about our fear of being ill-equipped, out of our depth, without even realising we were applying the very phenomenon we had witnessed on the beach. We were both feeling the same fears and anxieties – and we were being open with each other and talking about it.

It was a watershed moment for us. We realised that it wasn't a case of how much we knew; it was how much were we willing to be open, to listen and to learn. As long as we adopted the same honesty and openness as the people we were meeting, then we would be on solid ground.

A couple of weeks back, about two years after we filmed this pilot, Johnny and his partner attended Jules's yoga and cold dip class on the beach. It was so nice to see him again – a full-circle moment.

We can be a complicated bunch, us fellas, but I completely understood Mark's reasoning, and I was struck by how much thought he had put into the simple act of trying to get a group of guys together. It was quite overwhelming to see this huge group of lads laughing, catching up and enjoying each other's company. We felt humbled hearing Johnny Panchaud talk about his battles with addiction, or Johnnie McMillan, who spoke from the heart about being in such a dark place before he found this group.

I could see in Jules's eyes that he reminded her of our own son: broad shoulders, tall as a tree and a huge smile across his face. You will often hear people complaining that the next generation below them are too soft, that they need to toughen up. I honestly believe that to be total bollocks. My experience is that the next generation is smarter in so many ways than the one before it. We marvelled at these young men openly talking about their problems and challenges, in a direct and thoughtful way that we were too scared or unable to a mere twenty to thirty years earlier. Don't be fooled. Toughness comes in many forms. And silence about your emotional life tends not to be one of them.

BLUE BALLS

GREG

Meeting the Blue Balls on Portobello Beach in Edinburgh is something that I will never forget. The group's founder, Mark Miller, spoke very eloquently about what I would call: "The Trouble With Men". (My words, not his.)

Mark highlighted the reluctance of men of a certain age to gather in groups. I remember him saying that he always encouraged newcomers to arrive early, before the majority of the group had gathered, rather than at the allotted time when it could be a little anxiety inducing to turn the corner and be faced with fifty to a hundred men all laughing and chatting away.

This really hit home to me and made perfect sense. Jules and I had experienced something similar years before with our son Benny. In order to make him comfortable when he was little, we would always arrive early for kids' parties as then the group would build around the early birds, rather than have him arriving and standing in the door looking at a chattering throng of kids, already getting on like a house on fire.

3
THE TROUBLE WITH MEN

tailor-made for you.

I'm quite deep into this journey now and, like my yoga practice, I'm always open to individualised adjustments to hopefully make me feel better. But the one adjustment I hope YOU make (and I'll be right by your side) is a regular cold water dip/plunge/swim a few times a week. People will start to see you glow again, and you will start to feel stronger, like you have a purpose again, be proud of yourself and love yourself for the badass warrior you know you are. The beautiful thing about cold water dipping is if you close your eyes and imagine still doing this in your eighties and nineties, it should bring the broadest of smiles to your face! Look around at almost any swim group and you will see other swimmers at those ages, and they'll be smiling too.

SWIMMING PLAYLIST

'NIGHTSWIMMING'
R.E.M.

> **STAR SWIMMERS**
> ## THE NAIRN SELKIES
>
> We made our way down to the beach at Nairn to swim the Moray Firth with the Nairn Selkies. Their main reason for swimming was all the physical benefits. Shared among these selkie gals was a list of ailments, including nerve damage, hip replacements, fibromyalgia, rheumatoid arthritis, nerve pain, menopausal joint pain, all of which they said were soothed by regular sea swims in some pretty cold and unforgiving waters. This, we knew, was a tough gang of swimmers. The group's leader Marlene was hastily christened "The Sea Witch" for leading these hardy ladies into waters where we had to swim against regular rollers and quite a significant drag from the current. We felt in safe hands, but this was definitely one of our toughest swims.

women I have swum with, from the show's pilot to its second series, tell me that they have started to come back to feeling themselves by regularly dipping and getting into the water. From hot flushes to brain fog, mood changes, rubbish sleep patterns, feeling like you've lost yourself and your place in the world, the water somehow seems to be healing us and giving us a renewed sense of purpose.

I would emphasise, if this account of my own experience is resonating with you, try swimming or dipping with a group of women (although guys are welcome too) who are going through this fresh hell together. I know it can seem beyond daunting, but there is hope and laughter on the other side (and below the surface). I promise; I've seen it happen. Some women come out of this time, which is admittedly uniquely tough and challenging, stronger, sassier and truly excited to embrace this next chapter in their lives. Believe me, it's not over; there are ways you can unlock this new phase of your inner self.

If, like me, you are up for trying new ways to eat, taking supplements, trying every permutation of HRT out there (or not), moving your body as much as you can, positioning yourself into a downward dog, lifting weights, power walking and listening to every menopause podcast under the sun, I'm pretty sure you will get there and discover there is a coping strategy

MENOPAUSE CHAT

JULES

We felt it only right to give a mention to this as it's so central to my swimming experience, and as you can see from the show, I bring it up all the time!

Swimming and dipping have been invaluable in helping me navigate my way through the menopause. Personally, after a bad night's sleep (which can include nightmares, night sweats and anxiety), I know for a fact that if I am lucky enough to be able to get into the sea or my wee tub, then I will INSTANTLY feel better. The

---

STAR SWIMMERS
IMMERSE HEBRIDES

Jules got her menopause fix with the fine women of Immerse Hebrides. Off camera, she brain-drained her fellow menopausal women over Jammy Dodgers and tea, swapping tips and stories of how best to help themselves and each other. They all agreed that swimming went above and beyond in aiding them through this often difficult stage in their lives.

STAR SWIMMERS
THE MENOPAUSAL MERMAIDS

We were lucky enough to enjoy a swim with a group called the Menopausal Mermaids. Jules had got to know the Mermaids on Instagram and they'd kindly invited us along with them for a swim. These fun-loving women, who all met through the group, are the absolute embodiment of the "enjoy the ride" Helen Mirren quote. They are one committed bunch! Not only do they dip together every day, they also support each other year-round and go off on adventures together, including to Ireland and up and down the coasts of Scotland. They often have themed swim days featuring pirate excursions, 1950s-style parties and the like.

This is an incredible group of women, so welcoming to newbies. Jules became good friends with them and swims with them regularly. If you are new to the whole (peri)menopause experience, or struggling with it in any way, these gals are a fantastic point of contact if you are considering taking the plunge.

"LIFE DOESN'T END WITH MENOPAUSE; IT'S THE BEGINNING OF A NEW ADVENTURE. STRAP IN AND ENJOY THE RIDE!"

HELEN MIRREN

STAR SWIMMERS
ALICE GOODRIDGE

At the beautiful Loch Insh, a mile-long Highland loch with a fabulous activity centre located on its eastern shore, stands the Loch Insh Outdoor Centre, where we were off to swim with the Loch Insh dippers, set up by long-distance swimmer Alice Goodridge. Jules was excited to meet Alice as she had actually bought her book long before! Alice is known as the Sledgehammer Queen. She uses her eponymous heavy-duty implement to break the ice when needed, to ensure her swims are year-round and uninterrupted by the elements. Alice was seven months pregnant when we met her and that wasn't stopping her getting in the water every day. She said it was one of the things that made her feel like herself during her pregnancy, that swimming took all of her body's aches and pains away.

The immediately noticeable element about this friendly and welcoming swim group was the breadth of ages. Young to old, women mainly, all supporting each other, baking phenomenal chittery bites and counting an Irish mermaid among their ranks. Alice told us that although everyone in the group can swim at their own pace, she likes to push them to swim as far as they physically can. She is no pushover! For a more expansive look at swimming locations round Scotland, Alice's very well regarded book is worth a read. It's called *Swimming Wild in Scotland*, and you can pick it up online or at most bookstores.

FEELING AT HOME IN YOUR BODY

I know it's not going to be easy the very first time you take off the joggy bottoms and the big puffy coat and you are standing there stripped down to your swimming suit. (If you are wearing a bikini, put this book down, it's not for you! Only kidding; wear the bikini, you rock!) You might well feel very exposed, but please know this. Everyone else starts out feeling exactly the same way and, I promise you, the more you do it, the more you will start to enjoy some genuine body confidence. One reason being, you'll get a buzz that overrides any random worries about your wobbly bits. You'll start to see a change in how you carry yourself (and when you come out that baltic water, you'll be more concerned about getting yourself dry and cosy as quick as you can). I still can't believe that I go on the telly in my swimming suit. Don't get me wrong, I make sure I've shaved my legs and my bits, but I truly look at myself and know in my heart that I am more confident and carefree than I was before I swam.

SISTERS ARE DOING IT FOR THEMSELVES (AND THEIR HEALTH)

JULES

I would love women to not feel guilty for at least an hour a week, to set aside time for themselves, pack a bag with their swimming kit, go off and meet other people for a dip. Because I know for a fact that, even if it's raining, they're going to come back home feeling better. Women (you know it's true, guys) take the weight in the household more than guys, and I really believe it's vital they do something for themselves. Getting in that water, taking a few powerful breaths, will set you up for the rest of the day or even the week ahead, and you will be so proud of yourself, so energised, for doing that. I would also like women (and guys too) to take away from this book the knowledge that you are not past it. Take inspiration from the women we have met on our swimming show so far and know that you too have the potential to open yourself up to new adventures, new experiences and new feelings.

SWIMMING PLAYLIST

"ISLANDS IN THE STREAM"
BY KENNY ROGERS AND DOLLY PARTON

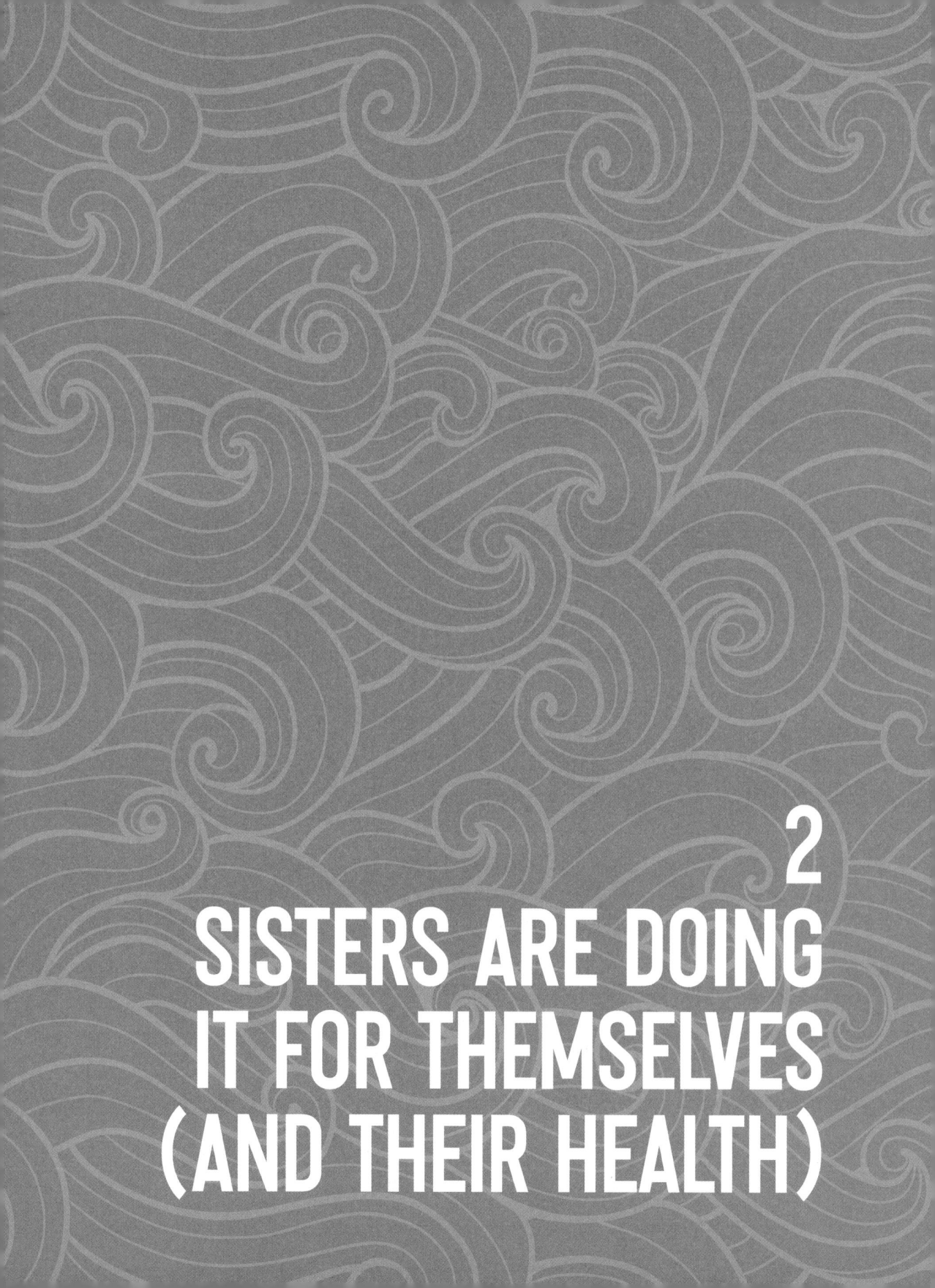

2
SISTERS ARE DOING IT FOR THEMSELVES (AND THEIR HEALTH)

A DOOK EVERY DAY KEEPS OLD AGE AT BAY

While research is still ongoing as to whether wild swimming helps you live longer, there is plenty of anecdotal evidence on hand to suggest it might. There are better informed people than us to talk you through the scientific physical benefits of this activity, but this much we do know: most of the older folks we have met on our wild swimming travels seem to say the same thing. The only thing that would stop them going in the water is becoming physically no longer capable of doing so.

STAR SWIMMERS
THE WILD HIGHLANDERS

The Wild Highlanders swimming group are a lovely bunch. And they count plenty of master swimmers among their number! We were very taken with Sandra, who, at eighty-three, was one of the oldest members of the group; but, as she told us herself, age really is just a number. Sandra learned to swim in the sea as a child and loved it, but she stopped swimming when she moved to Australia. When she hit sixty, she rediscovered her love for it and swims to this day. But Sandra doesn't just come for the swim. She comes to connect and be part of the community by participating in this group. Whatever their age, for so many people, these swimming groups lead to deep and meaningful friendships that last a lifetime. That sense of connection, which is often an intergenerational connection, is often the most important element of the activity.

Jules still talks about Sandra to this day. She is a wonderful inspiration to anyone who has trouble with sore joints, and especially for those women going through the menopause. Sandra told Jules, "You need to swim to keep strong and supple for the many years that lie ahead!"

SWIM SPOT

PINKSTON OUTDOOR POOL

Sandwiched between Possilpark, Sighthill and Springburn, this is a true urban swim. Pinkston was the old power station for the Glasgow trams. Now a legacy project following the 2014 Commonwealth Games, Pinkston is an incredible resource for people from all over the city to come and enjoy an outdoor swim at low cost. In the 1950s and 1960s, my grandad used to warn my father about the dangers of falling in the Maryhill canal, with its discarded shopping trollies and weird array of urban flotsam and jetsam, but now it's very clean, with a sand-filtered partition of the canal that, previously, we had no idea existed as a swimming location. Turns out that once upon a time Greg had filmed an episode of *Still Game* near here, in which Craig Ferguson's LA stuntman had returned to Glasgow and driven a car into the canal.

Kenny and his team discussed just how addictive cold water dipping is. For us, it was uplifting and emotional to spend time with a group of people who had replaced more toxic addictions with one so positive. Greg came out of the ice bath after eleven minutes and promptly devoured an impressive chittery bite (more on that later!): a dustbin-lid-sized waffle covered in chocolate. Meanwhile, Jules was lying in a sleeping bag shaking and pouring her heart out for the camera. Greg went to the stomach; Jules went to the heart.

It felt nice to walk on the extreme wild side with our newfound compadres. The ice bath approach is definitely not for everybody, but we would recommend trying it at least once! The crew went from thinking we were a couple of hippy actors in the grip of a new fad, to saluting us as a couple of Polar Bear badasses. We asked them if they would have had a shot if they had the time and unanimously they said, "No."

Since we completed filming, we have returned to the Polar Bears' new venue (they have moved from Finnieston to Bishopbriggs) for a second ice plunge. I hate to say it, but they're right: those freezing plunges become more and more addictive. Out of all the places we dipped in series one, the Polar Bear club is one of the most asked-for locations we visited.

COLD WATER THERAPY, ALSO KNOWN AS CRYOTHERAPY OR COLD-WATER IMMERSION, INVOLVES EXPOSING THE BODY TO COLD WATER, TYPICALLY BELOW 15°C. IT'S USED FOR VARIOUS REASONS, INCLUDING MUSCLE RECOVERY AFTER EXERCISE, REDUCING INFLAMMATION, IMPROVING CIRCULATION, AND BOOSTING MENTAL RESILIENCE. PRACTICES INCLUDE COLD SHOWERS, ICE BATHS, OUTDOOR SWIMS AND COLD-WATER IMMERSION THERAPY SESSIONS.

During the filming of the pilot, Jules linked up on Instagram with a young man called Aiden, who had been doing dips with a group called the Polar Bear Club. No prizes for guessing: those dips occurred in ice baths! Led by Kenny Neilson, the Polar Bears are a group mainly of recovering addicts. Jules was intrigued and enquired if they would not only like to appear in our programme but also kick off episode one.

It should be said that neither of us had taken an ice bath before, not even for ten seconds, let alone ten minutes. We were genuinely apprehensive. Bear in mind this was the very first swimming activity we were shooting for our opening series, and it was already far more extreme than any kind of dip or swim we had done to date. We had no idea what the outcome on camera was going to be. Tony, our director, was a bag of nerves. He was particularly worried about Jules. But when it came to ice baths, we couldn't have been in better hands than with Kenny and his team.

Their approach to getting into the water was far removed from ours. It was a fantastic learning experience to see how other people did it. We had always used yoga breathing to enter the water calmly and quietly, and we felt that getting out before you started shaking was important. Here, it was different. There was a much greater level of energy in the space. Kenny's team were all about boosting you in an extreme way but also supporting you through the group. It's important to stress that Jules and I never felt unsafe. They were continually taking our temperatures at our ears and the back of our necks, asking us if we were okay and generally making a fuss of us. Their approach was all-encompassing. Anything you felt, physically or emotionally, was encouraged out of you. For the Polar Bears, the ice bath was a weekly ritual that they referred to as a "reset". It clearly made sense in terms of the difficulties they all had encountered, and were still dealing with in their lives. This process tethered them like an anchor and gave them a sense of stability. The group took great pleasure in challenging each other to go further, push themselves and do more in the context of the ice bath. These challenges work: they can stay in the water for way longer than most people, and often enter competitions all over Europe. They have been known to take the plunge in a Thermo-Climatic Chamber in Krakow University, Poland, where the water temperature was as low as -50°C. (The only way to keep the water from freezing is to continually stir it.)

DOCTOR'S ORDERS

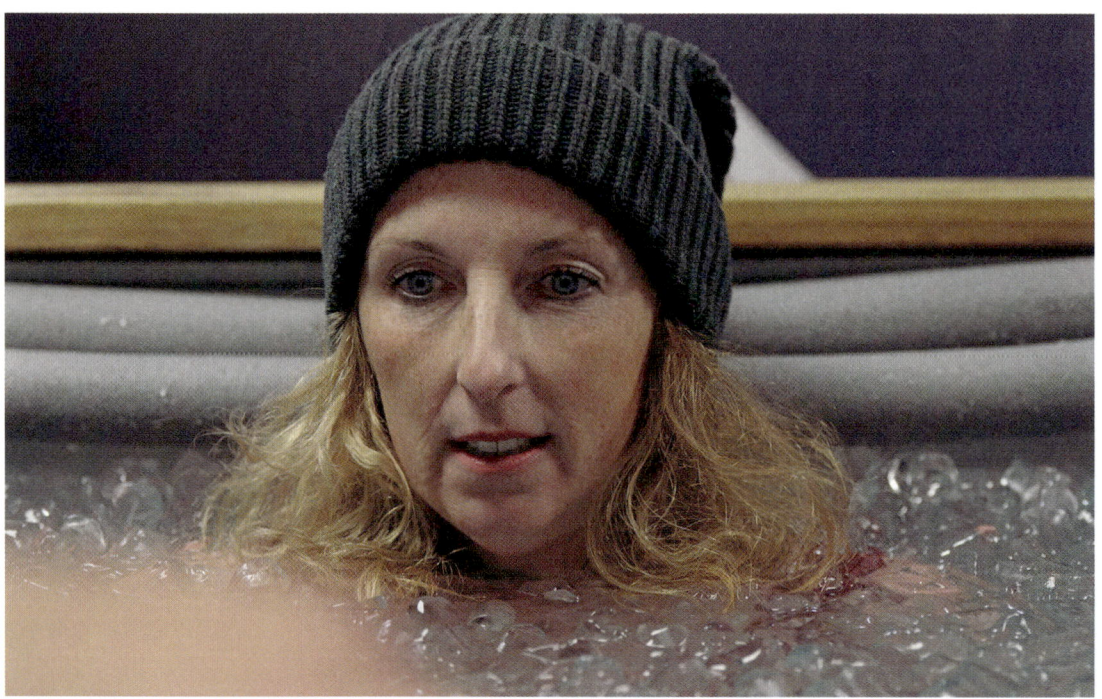

... AND COOLING DOWN AFTER!

Scotland has more water than it knows what to do with. We are lucky to have such a bountiful resource. It has been said that if you stretch out all of Scotland's coastline, it would be as long as the Eastern Seaboard of the United States. We have many different types of bodies of water in Scotland, and we thought it seemed apt to try and get a taste of all of them.

Greg and I feel very strongly that wild swimming is an inclusive endeavour, not some expensive pastime for the well-to-do. Because we spent many years living in a city, we wanted from the get-go to explore areas around us, places that people could reach for the price of a bus trip. The very first group of swimmers we encountered could not have been more urban.

THE BOOKSHELF

THE LIFELINE
BY LIBBY PAGE

because spending time in a sauna helps to relax you, and studies have shown that saunas can help with depression as they can have the same effect as an anti-depressant.

A sauna brings people together, creating the social benefits of connection and being part of a community. We have noticed more and more community sauna "boxes" springing up, and these could and should be accessible and affordable for everyone. They can offer, too, a perfect tie-in with cold water dipping.

We know that a lot of people might think saunas aren't for them – we were the same but now can't get enough of their friendly, relaxing vibe – but of course, if you have any health worries, check with your doctor first. As long as you remember to stay hydrated before, during and after your sauna and tie it in with a dip, you will reap so many benefits of hot and cold therapy. Always listen to your own body, and be aware that some folk like to stay in longer than others. Greg and I tend to do ten to fifteen minutes of heat followed by no more than three minutes in the cold water. A bit like when you first join a gym, there is nearly always someone on hand to offer you a wee bit of advice and assistance if you are unsure or have any questions.

GETTING HOT . . .

Of course, you can always combine the experience of cold water swimming with the pleasures of a lovely warm sauna! There are multiple benefits to moving between the hot and cold of outdoor water and a sauna: you can think about this process as being like an intravascular workout; it's basically akin to a gym session for your arteries as they expand and contract going between the two different temperatures. Combining cold water therapy and saunas is beneficial to both your physical and mental health. For physical health, it can improve your cardiovascular health, it can lower your blood pressure, it can reduce the risk of cardiovascular disease, and it can help with cardiorespiratory fitness.

And, of course, saunas alone are hugely beneficial. Some even have their own cold water plunge pools, so you can shirk the chilly outdoors loch experience if you choose . . . Taking saunas can reduce inflammation throughout your body, they are good for your muscles, they can help them grow and they increase the blood flow in your muscles, which is good for recovery. Saunas also help to boost immunity by increasing white blood cell production. In addition, saunas can be amazing for mental health because they can reduce stress, the heat from a sauna can trigger the release of endorphins which have mood-boosting and stress-reducing effects. Saunas can also improve your sleep

SWIM SPOT

EAST NEUK OF FIFE

After a lifetime of living in Glasgow, we moved to the East Neuk of Fife. The East Neuk is a place we had brought our kids to for many years and now is a clear contender for the dipping capital of Scotland. For those that don't know this part of the world, it's just over the Queensferry Crossing from the south and turn right, basically. A beautiful string of villages including Lower and Upper Largo, Elie, St Monans, Pittenweem, Anstruther and round finally to St Andrews. When you've lived the majority of your time in Glasgow, it's easy to confuse perpetual West Coast wetness with the whole of Scottish weather, but in our experience, the east coast, though often a couple of degrees cooler, always seems to be slightly drier than what we are used to in the well-washed city of Glasgow.

We met up with Lara Brown of the Seafield Sinkers, a Facebook community of over a thousand swimmers. Lara's enthusiasm for wild swimming is infectious, and she was a pleasure to hang out with. Positioned in front of an old salt mill, the St Monans tidal pool is a little different from the Pittenweem one. Owing to the height of the surrounding wall, it only changes water at the new and full moon, as opposed to twice a day with the tides at Pittenweem. This unusual feature means the water at this tidal pool is slightly warmer. If you're put off by the cold, why not try a tidal pool like St Monans – it's good to ease yourself in!

DOCTOR'S ORDERS

JULES'S HATS OBSESSION

I was lucky enough to have been sent two beautiful floral swim hats, reminiscent of what Esther Williams might have worn to match her glamorous swimsuits in an aquamusical. Having done some research on Sian, I found out she used to be a florist and is also an artist. My notion was to introduce Sian to these fabulous hats as I felt they were meant to be together. The minute I saw her smiling face, I knew this super cool retro swimming cap had found a new home. She really suited it, and we had a laugh wearing them together and swimming out into the sea loch. If you do get the chance to visit Loch Eynort, remember to take your binoculars – as well as your glam swimcap – as it is a well-known location to spot seals.

At Loch Eynort, a sea loch in Shetland, we met lovely Sian, an islander who had returned home in 2020. Sian and Max had felt the stress of living in the city and took the opportunity to escape back to where they knew. We felt compelled to ask Sian as a journalist what she thought about the wild swimming craze. It was a question at the forefront of our minds all the way through filming series two. Was this just some passing trend, like hipster beard oils, the Ice Bucket Challenge or those TikTok dances all the kids were doing in the pandemic? Sian was of the opinion that wild swimming is here to stay. Because it's, let's be honest, very addictive, because it helps to calm people with anxiety, because you are out in nature, because it is free. Really, then, why would you stop doing it? She makes a good case for it. And we've been at it five years now, which for us is a long trend, but I guess – as with everything – time will tell.

SWIM SPOT

SLIGACHAN BRIDGE, SKYE

Sligachan Old Bridge, on the Isle of Skye, is a fantastic swim spot. Listen, we're not ones for mindlessly drinking in ancient folklore, but if you tell us there's a chance at eternal beauty if you dook yer head for seven seconds in the river below this famous bridge and let it dry off naturally, you can bet your arse we're daein' it. Why wouldn't you? Think about it. If it's not true, no harm done. You have a frozen head for a few seconds. But what if it IS true? Why would you pass up that lottery ticket? So we all dooked. So did Bonnie and our entire crew.

The Egyptians did it, the Romans did it, the Greeks did it and us Scots have always done it, but somewhere along the timeline of our history (possibly when the boom in cheap flights to Spain started in the 1950s), we stopped. And then, during the Covid lockdowns of the early 2020s, when we had to find things to do on our doorstep, and preferably outside, while examining our own mental and physical wellbeing, wild swimming resurfaced with a vengeance. Certainly, that's when it started to become part of our lives. Now we are mirroring the passion of the Scandi countries where younger generations in countries like Finland and Norway seem to be embracing wellness traditions. On a recent trip to Oslo we were both struck by the sheer number of groups booking community sauna and Fjord dip sessions as part of their weekly routines. These community saunas are regular gathering places for young and old folk alike, to spend time together and catch up.

THE LESSER KNOWN ISLE OF SKYE

Skye was the first island we visited on our swimming adventures, and we would thoroughly recommend you visit, if you haven't already. There are so many locations on this island we could have filmed an entire series here alone, so get yourselves there and start exploring! Accommodation is competitive in the summer months, and no special case was made for our shoot. We were all spread out and scattered to the four corners of the Isle. We found ourselves at a place called The Braes, looking over to the Isle of Raasay. Now, this might have been in the busiest season for tourist traffic, but you'd never have known it here. We didn't see another soul the entire time we stayed in this wee haven. We would walk down to the local beach and have it all to ourselves. Only a couple of sheep for company. Even at a time when the island is creaking under the weight of its most intense few months of influx, you can still find spots that appear abandoned. With an ever-changing backdrop of jaw-dropping scenery, Skye is an incredible island to explore for wild swims. It truly has the goods. And who you gonna call if you want to go a little more off grid? That's right. Our good friend Matt!

DOOK / DOOKIN
"Dook" means to dip, and "dookin" refers to the act of dipping into the water, such as swimming in a loch or the sea.

People through the ages have come here to these pools to heal themselves. This shows that cold water swimming, though enjoying a renaissance, is not some passing fad or hipster invention. It's been around for a very long time. The Gaelic translation for Loch Seunta is "The Magical Loch"; and we were certainly getting swept up in its magic – even to set eyes on the otherworldly colour of the water felt transporting for us. A little nondescript body of water without any particularly stunning views proved to be one of the most exhilarating and memorable dips we ever had. Don't judge a swim by its cover!

Let's be clear here: to our eyes, no one partaking of this modern trend is laying claim to the invention of open water swimming. It seems more likely that it simply has skipped a couple of generations before bouncing back. We often meet older folk who like to say, "When I was young we just used to call it swimming" – and of course, they're right, as are the many older folk we've spoken to who remember splashing about the tidal pools of the East Neuk or elsewhere when they were little.

There are so many benefits to wild swimming – that's what this whole book is about. We'll start with the most obvious: it's great for your health. Maybe exercise isn't your bag – we certainly don't consider ourselves to be gym rats – but hear us out. We're not asking you to swim across the Channel. You don't even have to swim at all, really – you can just dook (that's "going for a dip" if you're not from Scotland). Even immersing yourself in the waters of wild swimming for a short time will do you good.

A THERAPY AS OLD AS TIME

It might seem like wild swimming is this new, modern craze, but it's more likely to have been around since the dawn of time – as shown by ancient rock art in the Cave of Swimmers in the Sahara Desert. They didn't have heated pools back in the olden days, and that didn't stop them!

Take Loch Seunta, also known as the Healing Pool, in Skye. Our friend Matt took us for a swim there, and it was one of our favourite swims for many reasons. Firstly, we never would have found this spot if it weren't for the local knowledge of Matt, our guide. Secondly, and perhaps weirdly, this spot wasn't much to look at. It looked like a small hole in the ground surrounded by reeds. Not particularly picturesque and not helped by the filthy weather lashing us on a cold August afternoon on Skye while we were filming *Jules & Greg's Wild Swim*. But here's the thing about the Healing Pool Matt explained: the water flows from a ground fissure and it takes hundreds of years to arrive here through the depths of the cascading rock formations of the Quiraing, with the water not seeing daylight for its entire journey until it reaches its final destination. Matt told us that this was a winter swim smack bang in the middle of the summer. He tried to warn us about how cold it was going to be, but we didn't care. In we went. Holy cow. Swimming in 8°C when everywhere else is at 15°C or 16°C was positively surreal.

1
DOCTOR'S ORDERS

WELCOME

OUTTAKES

Jules remembers the horror of getting changed into her episode outfit in the back of the van in a full car park at the Co-op. This is the stuff you don't see. That and the crew scrambling around looking for coins so they can go to the toilet.

WHAT YOU'LL GET OUT OF THIS BOOK

We hope that you get out of this book what we have been getting out of wild swimming for the last few years: an amazing new hobby. (If you don't already do it.) Tips and advice on where to do it, opportunities to join new social circles and make new pals, a new and real sense of achievement and adventure, a second childhood, a fresh outlook on life perhaps, and hopefully a few laughs. The thing we would love the most is if you took all the advice found in these pages, drew a deep breath and gave it a go!

WELCOME

It felt like the end of summer camp. (Though, as Jules observed, "Only you felt this, Greg, because you're a Canuck freak. Nobody else knows what summer camp feels like.") It was like no one wanted to say goodbye; in a short time, we had formed some very strong bonds. Just like when you're in a swimming group. We all left each other really hoping that the good vibes we felt we had captured on camera would emerge and an audience would feel them too. We also knew that TV timescales when it comes to decisions always seem to take an age, which meant we now faced a waiting game. The pilot wouldn't be transmitted for six months, and it probably would be another four months after that before a decision was made.

And of course that decision was that our wild swim adventure would become a series ...

you and says, "I had a look at the GoPro. Well done. Great footage!"

It was important to us that the camera came into the water with us (rather than filming us from the shores) for a couple of reasons. We wanted the audience to feel that they were coming in and swimming with us; plus, we thought it was a particularly interesting aspect of Scottish scenery that felt like it hadn't been shown before. What does Scotland look like from the water? The hills and Munros look even more dramatic as they loom up behind us. Underwater filming also gives a better sense of what the challenges of Scottish swimming look like. Plenty of times Jules and I would surface only to be slapped hard in the face by a wind-driven wave on a loch. But from the shore, the water looks much calmer and kinder.

Gullane Beach was the site of our crew's first communal swim. We even managed to persuade our director, Tony, to join in. What happened with our crew is something we have seen throughout the wild swimming community. There are people who watch and you can tell they are curious and keen to give it a try, but for whatever reason, they are cautious. We saw that with our crew that week. No one went into the water apart from us and Sean, but by the end of the week, our director, our producer, our soundman Colin, and our researcher Rowan all took the plunge with us.

(Greg: By the way, Jules bought us all fish and chips from the famous Atlantis fish and chips stand. I'm mentioning this because she's too modest to pipe up about it herself. Thanks, Jules!)

feeling of *we are all in this together*. It's just brilliant!

Filming that pilot was so special and always will be because it was the first thing we shot. In telly, things are often shot out of sequence, so this was an unusual case. It was so lovely to see Tony, our director, Jim, our producer and our whole crew capture that sense of incredible tranquillity and togetherness that morning. They got to see what we loved, and they chatted to everyone after the shoot, and that's what we wanted the show to be. Tony managed to capture that feeling of community and togetherness on camera; he got into the swimmers' stories with a real sense of care and love. We thought, if we can keep this vibe going, hopefully viewers will want to get in the water – and, hopefully, we'll achieve that same goal with this book and encourage you to dip your toe in, if you haven't already.

LIFE IMITATES ART

The last day of filming on the pilot, our director had the idea for us to round the show off by swimming solo at Gullane Bay. It was the most beautiful day, and we lay on the beach with our dog, Bonnie, as we completed an exhausting week. Ironically, we were finishing up our pilot about cold water swimming on what felt like the hottest day of the year. We really could have been in the South of France. Except when we got in the water, of course. That's the strange thing about our show: sometimes on camera it can look as if the water is warm and inviting, just as it would be in real life, but in reality, it's bloody cold and takes a bit of tenacity getting used to it.

At Gullane, we had the whole beach to ourselves. We spent the afternoon filming underwater shots with Sean, our cameraman. He has such an amazing eye and gets you to do things like dives and swim-bys that end up looking amazing in the final edit. Sean is one of us: he actively participates in every swim we do. With a camera over his shoulder, lining up shots in very cold water is not easy, but Sean never complains. Once we are in the water, time starts ticking: we get cold so quickly that there is no time to do reshoots or extend the filming time beyond fifteen minutes or so. There can be no requests from Sean along the lines of: "Great swimming. Any chance you can swim back and swim towards me again?" He will also use a waterproof GoPro to film us underwater. He'll sometimes throw it to us and we become his camera assistants. It always feels good when he comes to

WELCOME

JULES

Life is so strange sometimes. I would never have thought on the day we shot the opening of our pilot for *Jules & Greg's Wild Swim* down on the shores of beautiful Loch Lomond, with Natalie and a class full of her regulars, plus some of our family, that it would lead to Gayle saying, "Why don't you sign up to do a yoga course?"

Even stranger, I said yes. I did the course – and loved it! – and now I take people into the water. I get to see what Natalie was seeing: the changes in people, how it helps them focus, relax, but mostly just feel better. It's a real privilege that they join the group and give themselves over to the experience and let me guide them in through breathwork. There's a real in my trunks doing yoga. I'll feel like an interloper. Do ANY guys go? They'll all be looking at me." I should also mention that she's very good at dropping a truth bomb on you. "Greg, no one gives a shit. No one cares, literally. They're not there to check you out. They're there for themselves. Get over yourself." Direct hit. It always makes me howl with laughter when she gives me a two-footed dose of reality. It's one of the many reasons why I love her.

One of the other reasons is that she rarely gives up on people, and she never gave up on me. But she's a proud woman, and she wasn't going to beg. If I was going to come and have this experience, I was going to have to "get over myself" and get in the car. So, in the end, I did.

I remember acting like an annoying seven-year-old on the way to Luss. "Do people have heart attacks doing this? People drown in Scottish lochs all the time. Is the yoga hard? How long do I have to stay in the water for?" It's actually a miracle that she didn't pull over and leave me at the side of the road. When we got there, people could not have been friendlier or more welcoming. No fuss, just a sense of calm and tranquillity. I sat on a yoga mat and stared over to Ben Lomond, but at the back of my mind, my eyes kept flicking to the freezing water. "I'm going in that." Jules could see I was nervous, but her smile and her constant squeezing of my hand told me I would be okay.

Our instructor Natalie told us that going into cold water was like holding a mirror up to yourself. People come out giddy, laughing, crying. Whatever was going on inside your head and body would come out in a very weird and wonderful way. Great, I thought. A new anxiety! What if I get in this water and it's like a public therapy couch? What if I start bawling my eyes out and start babbling instructions to everybody to "go hug your mothers while you still can!"

In I went. Down to my neck on an exhale breath. Never felt cold like it. But I didn't feel a sense of panic or the urge to run out the water. After thirty seconds, a calm washed over me as my core fired up like a furnace. It was pure gentle meditation. It's genuinely difficult to describe. I'm not a religious person, not at all, but I wondered if this was what it felt like to get baptised. Who knows? I was just a baby so I don't remember. (But I think the water was cold that day too.) I thought about my brothers, my mother and my father, Jules and my boys. This overwhelming feeling of tranquillity hit me. Utter micro focus and peace of mind.

I knew in an instant that everything – and I mean everything – was going to be all right.

What a gift, Jules! I feel so lucky that in my fifties I have found a new joyful and shared hobby with my partner. It's so, so easy after many years of being together for couples to do their own thing. It's so easy to slide towards separate lives as marriage moves through the years. There are times where it must happen to every couple. But for me, it's much more fun doing things together, and now we had this really intense and cool shared experience. I will always be grateful to Jules for introducing me to something that hopefully I will still be doing (with her!) when I'm ninety-nine. Thanks, doll!

WELCOME

gather on Zoom most weeks. Huddled together on a computer screen in grief, we would laugh and reminisce. We were now solely responsible for fostering our family ties in the absence of Ma.

Whisky had also become my chosen form of anaesthesia. I would drink with my brothers, say goodnight to them, have another couple of drams and fall asleep on the sofa. It seemed like a harmless enough habit, but over time it was starting to worry Jules. "Hey. I need you healthy and so do your boys," she'd try and tell me. I would shrug her concern off, make a joke and sweep it under the carpet. Meanwhile she had regularly started attending this thing called Soulful Sunday. Every week she would sign me up and every Sunday morning I would postpone, with a rotating bunch of excuses. "I have a cold. Too tired. Too shy. Too many whiskies last night." If I'm honest, it was actually always the last excuse; the others were a bullshit cover for the inconvenient truth.

I started to notice just how happy Jules was on her return from these classes. She was literally glowing, and while she enjoyed the occasional drink, she was teetotal on a Saturday night because she wasn't going to miss her Sunday morning dip for anything. Over the space of a short few months, a little schism had nestled in between us. She was happy in Loch Lomond with her pals, and I was happy in my whisky bubble.

Jules is adorable. And she is relentless in her encouragement of me to try new things. Every week she would patiently ask if I wanted to join her, and every week I made my polite excuses. I was being such a bloke about it. "Yeah, dunno if I fancy standing on a beach with forty women

GREG

My introduction to cold water swimming was completely down to Jules. I wanted to share it with you because this relatively new (to so many other than the diehards) pastime seems to skew so female. Guys, it seems, can be just that little bit more reticent to jump in – and I was no different.

It was a strange year, 2019. *Still Game* had finished for good after twenty-odd years; we had moved to California and the pandemic was just around the corner. At the beginning of 2020, Covid was beginning to rear its ugly head and we found ourselves back in the UK. (Isn't it strange how it all seems so recent and yet so distant at the same time? In the last five years, I struggle to remember whether certain things happened three months ago or two years ago. It was a time when time itself seemed to concertina and stretch in the weirdest ways.)

It's fair to say, I was feeling a little bit directionless – actually, I was more than a bit lost. To compound this feeling, both my mum and dad, Anne and Eddie, had passed away within seven months of each other in 2018. I've heard it said that there is your life before your parents pass and your life after, and I felt that so acutely.

My two brothers live quite far away: Tony in Cornwall and Steve in Vancouver. I used to hear how they were doing from my mum, who was the family fulcrum, and thanks to her my brothers and I only needed to catch up infrequently. With Mum's passing, that all changed. With her no longer around to fulfil that go-between updating role, my brothers and I would

WELCOME

OUR FIRST WILD SWIM – WHERE IT ALL BEGAN

JULES

One day, my pal Gayle called me up and said, "Do you want to come for a dip with me in Loch Lomond?"

I was really nervous. It used to take me ten minutes to get myself into 25°C-water on holiday. How was I going to cope with water temperatures below 15°C?

Gayle was similarly nervous, but we took each other's hands and got in the water together. Laughing, screaming and chittering, we were so proud of ourselves for having done it. As we were walking back to our cars, Gayle mentioned there was a woman called Natalie Valenti, a yoga instructor, who was leading a class on the beach, after which she took you for a dip.

"I'm intae it," I said, and Gayle booked us in that night.

Next thing I know, I'm standing on a yoga mat on the shores beneath Ben Lomond, attending my first ever "Soulful Sunday". Gayle and I were welcomed into the small group, and we both soon realised that Natalie was an amazing teacher. She had started the class because she had been suffering from anxiety and wanted to do something outdoors. She was looking for something – wellness, peace of mind, confidence . . . you know what I mean. She and her friends had found it in the water, and before too long she was down there weekly.

This experience was nothing short of transformative for me. The feeling of well-being after being in cold water is difficult to describe, but I'll do my best here in this book with the help of our new swimming pals. The science behind it is fairly well documented, but until you experience it, you don't fully understand it. All I knew was that I was *hooked*.

wild swimming community and its seemingly infinite set of reasons for loving cold water. Just like on the shores of Loch Ness itself, we were very quickly in deep and absolutely loving it.

During the shoot, we were finding that the show isn't about us – it's about the people we dip and swim with. We were dying to hear their stories: how they had got here? And why were they still doing it? What keeps them sticking on their layers and getting into freezing cold rivers, lochs, even the sea – we had started to get nosy and wanted more! It's become addictive, finding out other people's stories. We are actors, after all; we genuinely love talking to people, hearing the before and afters of dipping and swimming in their lives, and tuning in to why they can't get enough of it. Really, with that dip in Loch Ness, we had just got started.

They say that changing people's habits in the short term is easy. Changing people's habits over the *long* term is the challenge. We are, it seems, hard-wired in Scotland to be fearful of our surrounding waters. Those waters are cold, they are dangerous. While these things cannot and should not be ignored, neither should the benefits and rewards. We seem to be learning from our Nordic neighbours that this cold swimming pastime can be hugely beneficial to our physical and mental health. So far, what we are seeing through our TV show is that cold water therapy is here to stay.

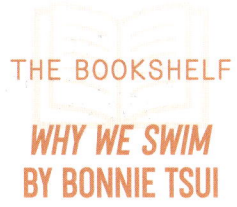

THE BOOKSHELF

WHY WE SWIM
BY BONNIE TSUI

Let us make the case for why you should try this nutty pastime by telling you all about the incredible benefits of wild swimming, how it improves so much in life from your health to your relationships. But best of all, we want to tell you about some of the wonderful people we have met – and continue to meet! – along the way. If you don't want to listen to us, then perhaps you might be glad to listen to them! Perhaps you will find that you have more in common with this burgeoning wild swimming community than you thought.

TAKING WILD SWIMMING ON THE ROAD

That weekend up at Loch Ness, we'd been wild swimming for a year or so and we had noticed the change in each other. More happiness, more smiles, more laughter and, after more than twenty years of marriage, we had found a hobby that we loved to do together. And we knew that wild swimming has also been a revelation for many others across Scotland – that's why we made our TV show, *Jules & Greg's Wild Swim*, to hear other people's stories and understand their motivations for getting in that water just like us: hip replacements, inflammation, menopause, mental health, grief, stress, just to skim the surface. We had accidentally happened across this

WELCOME

After about ten minutes (more than enough at that time of year!), we finally got out and quickly towelled ourselves down. The beach was filling up with groups of women, laughing, chatting and getting ready to go in. We realised that we had stumbled across a (very cold) hot spot. We were still buzzing from our swim and our chat with our fellow cold dippers, when on our way to the car, we were stopped by two tourists from Bilbao. We thought they were going to ask us about Loch Ness, the history, the scenery, the monster. But all they wanted to know was: *what the hell possessed you to strip off and enter this freezing loch?*

Good question.

The simple answer is that it feels amazing, plus it comes with so many benefits. The longer, more complicated answer – well, that's why you're reading this book.

We're pretty confident you didn't get it to look at pictures of the two of us in our bathing suits. Scratch that, *supremely* confident. Maybe you are curious to see what all the fuss is about. Maybe it was a rubbish Christmas present and it's been gathering dust on your shelf for a while. But right now, this book is in your hands for a reason. Maybe you're thinking about taking the plunge yourself? We suspect so.

DIPPING INTO A NEW ADVENTURE

We know what you're thinking – what makes two actors qualified to talk to you about wild swimming? Well, we're not exactly new to this. One chilly September morning in 2021, a trip to visit a pal in Inverness would reveal itself to be a totally transformative, life-changing event for both of us. We didn't know it yet, but that day would lead us on an unforgettable journey across the wild waters of Scotland – from its magnificent lochs and rivers to its rugged coastlines – and into the world of wild swimming.

On that weekend, we acted on a recommendation off our friend to head home to Glasgow via Dores Beach on the northern shore of Loch Ness. Other than a few dog walkers, we had the whole place to ourselves. We stripped down to our suits right there on the freezing cold pebbles and entered the water. (Jules still has a video of this dip.) The loch was dark brown and, within ten feet of the shore, we were out of our depth in very cold water. It was a little unnerving, but we felt safe because we were together. We made pals with a family of ducks who swam over to check out these two idiots; it was easy to interpret their noisy quacks as laughter, but we weren't caring.

WELCOME

WHO WE ARE

Hello! We're Jules and Greg. If you picked this book up because you enjoyed our TV show about wild swimming, or are maybe wondering what this cold water swimming thing is all about, then let's start at the beginning. Below is the mantra Jules was taught by her pal Natalie Valenti down at Luss by Loch Lomond, the first time she took her in, then Greg heard it when he went in and we still use it to this day to not only get ourselves in, but to help others in, especially those who might be trying cold water swimming for the first time. So let's steel ourselves, take a deep breath and try something new together . . .

"You are about to go into the water for the first time. It's going to be bloody cold, but if you follow this simple routine, you will find it a little easier. Make a fist with your right hand. Bring your fist up to your chest. Now bring your left hand up beside your fist in an open palm . . . Now take the clenched fist and firmly press it against the flat palm. Bring your shoulders down. Use your middle finger to tap your nose and inhale deeply through your nostrils and exhale through a tight mouth like you're blowing through a straw. Inhale deeply once more and on the next exhale, in we go . . ."